D1524567
ANIMALS
DOT MARKERS
ACTIVITY BOOK
FROM THE TEAM AT
SLINKY
SLOTH

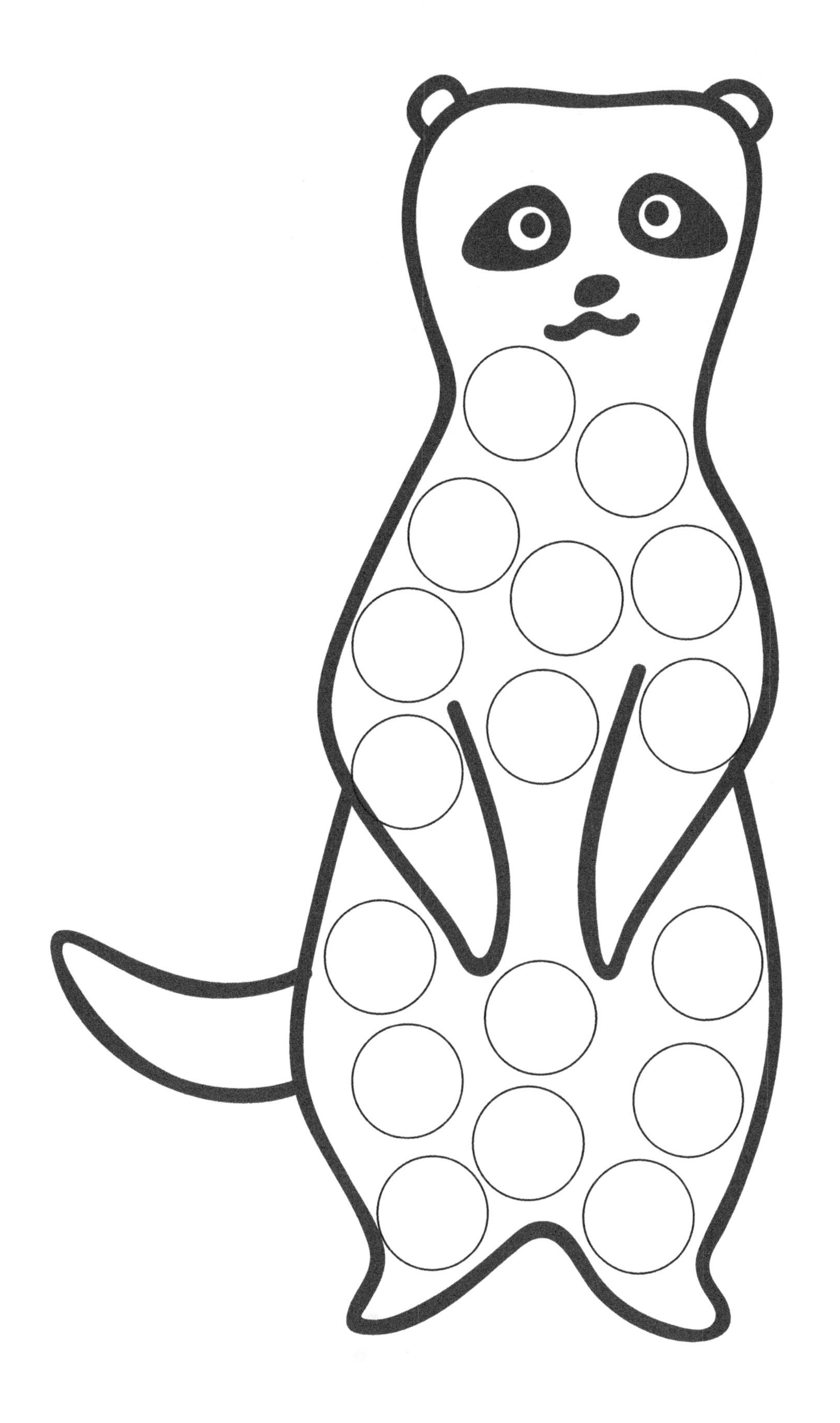

meerkat

frog

bear

kangaroo

goat

horse

chicken

armadillo

snail

eagle

fox

camel

ant

duck

bat

gecko

dragonfly

gorilla

butterfly

owl

parrot

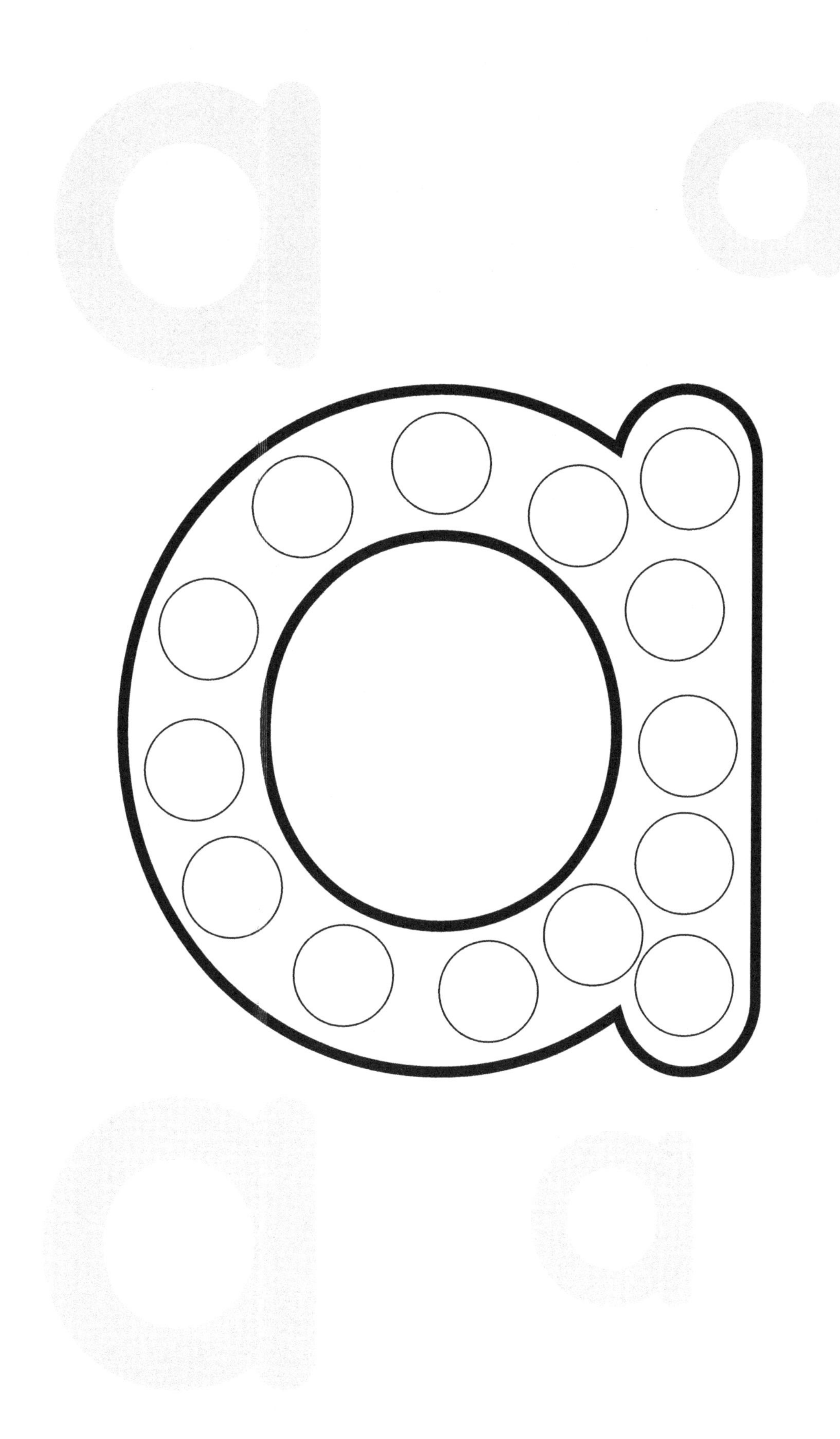

SLINKY
SLOTH

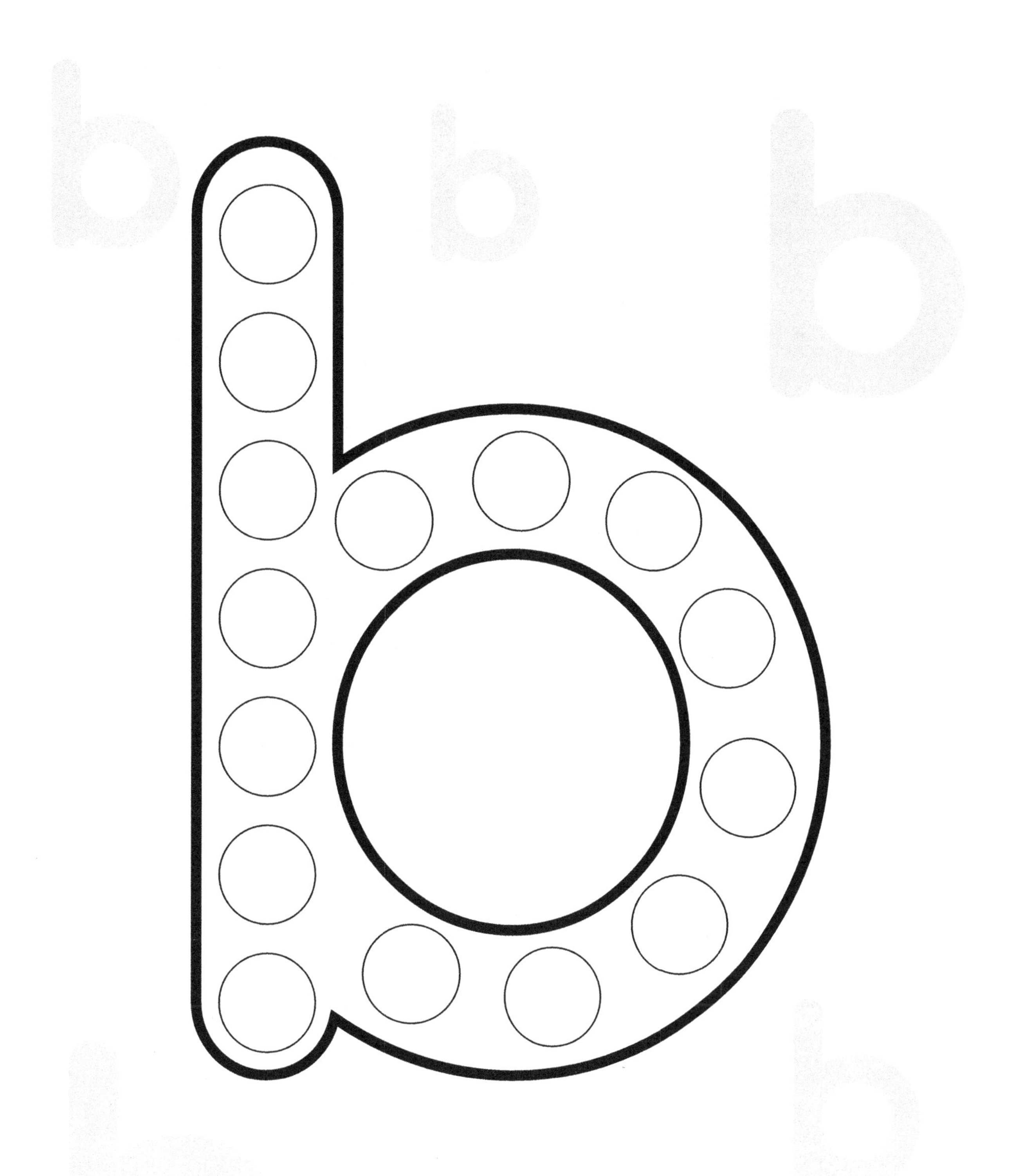

SLINKY
SLOTH

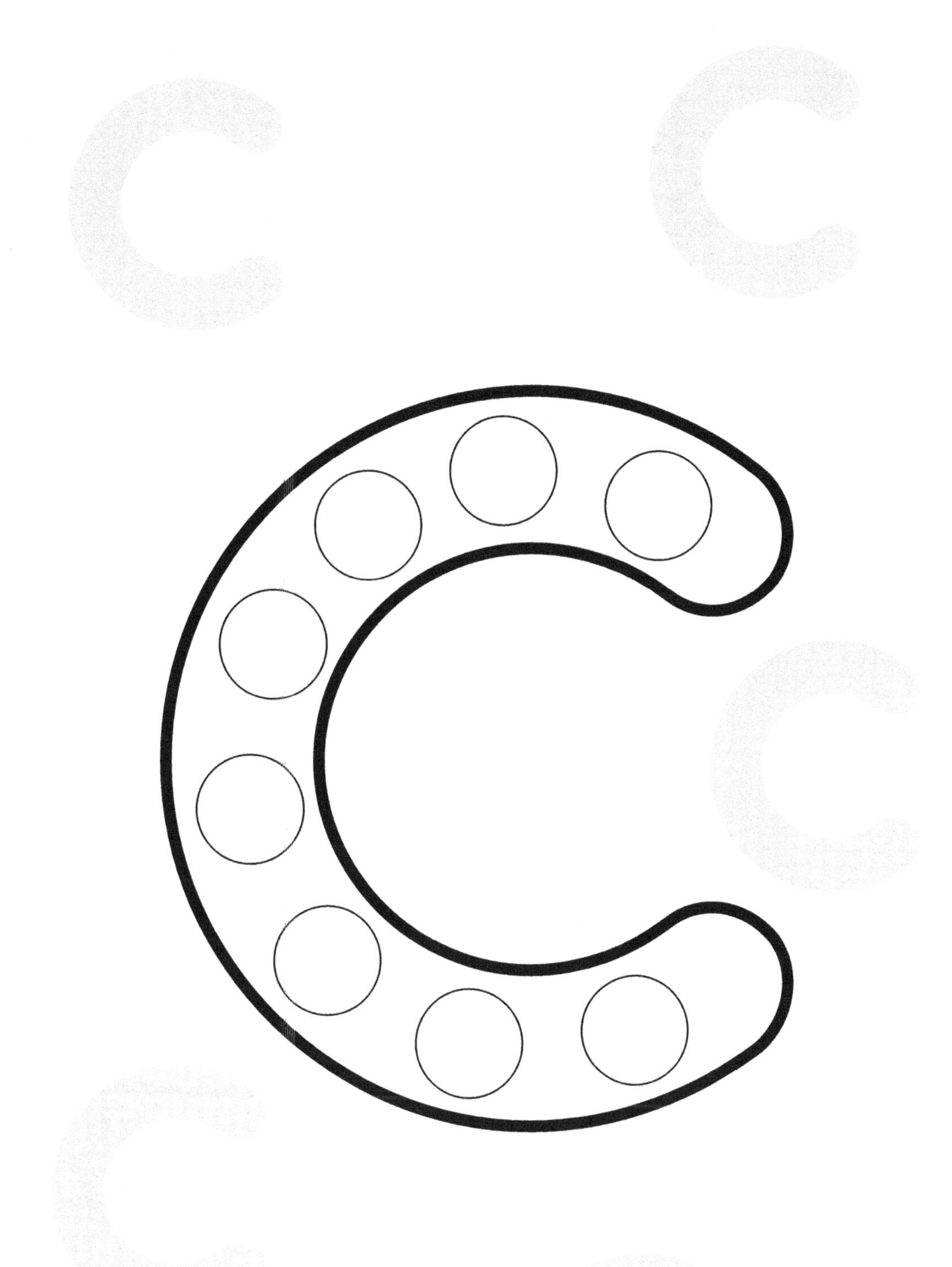

SLINKY
SLOTH

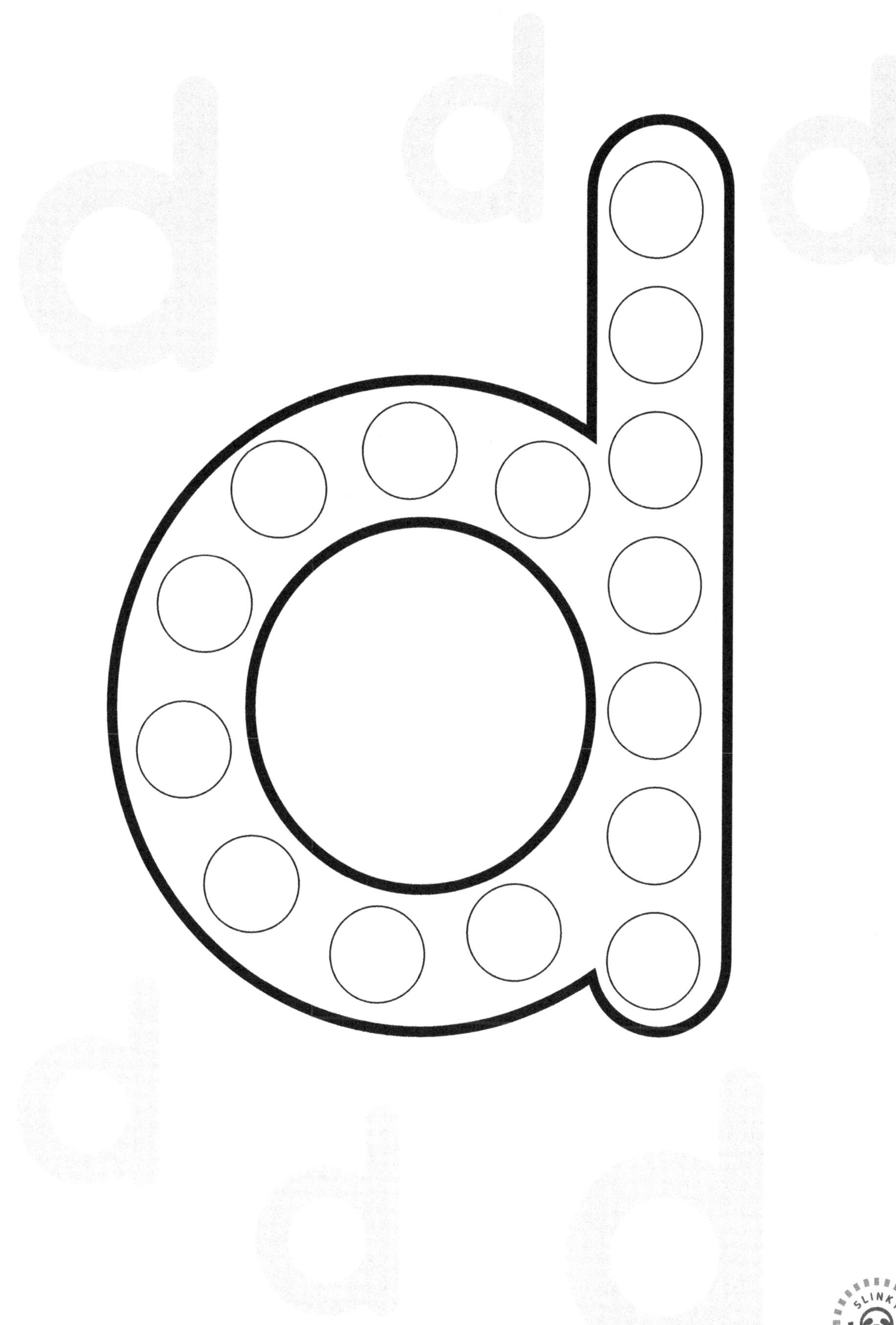

SLINKY
SLOTH

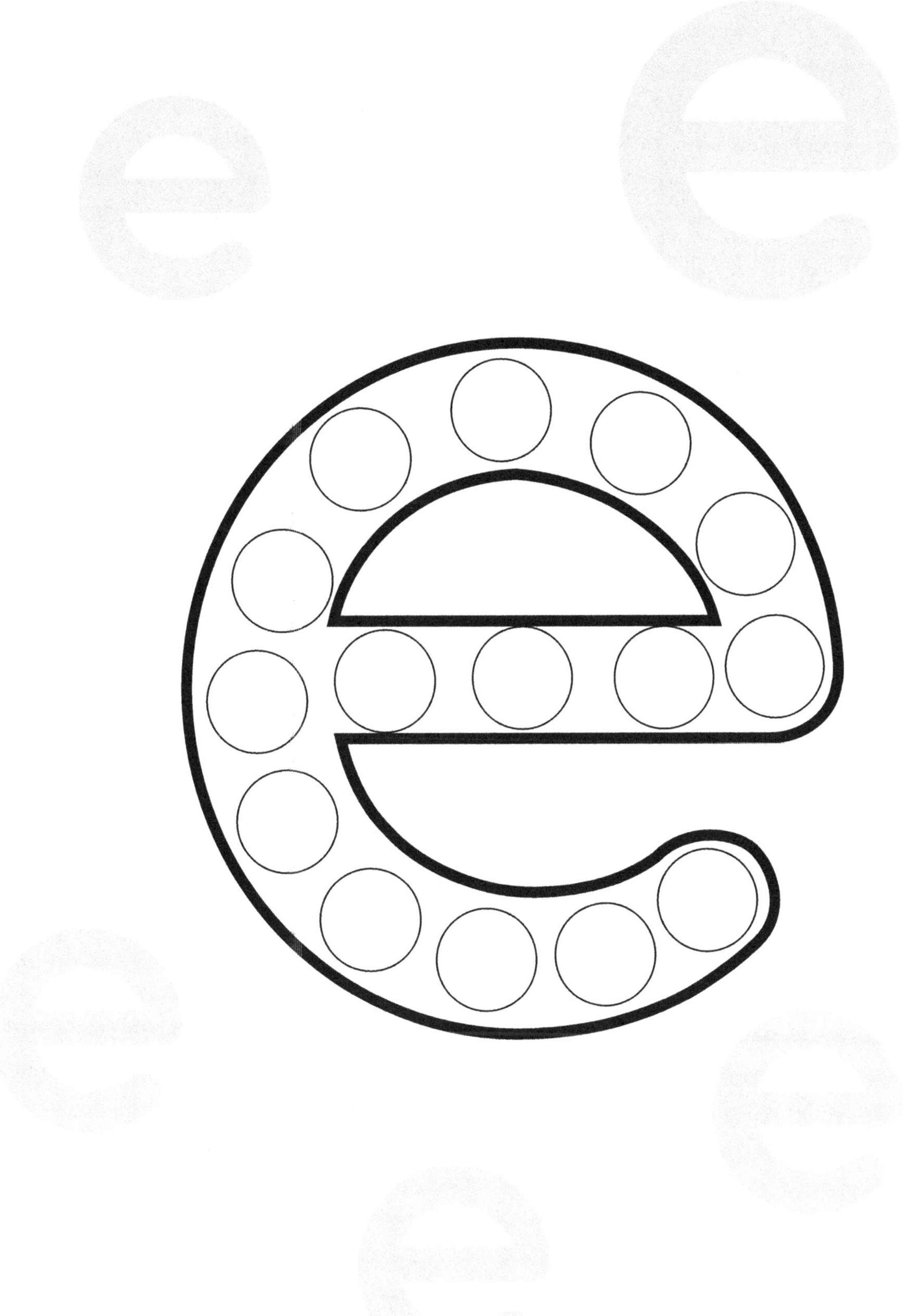

SLINKY
SLOTH

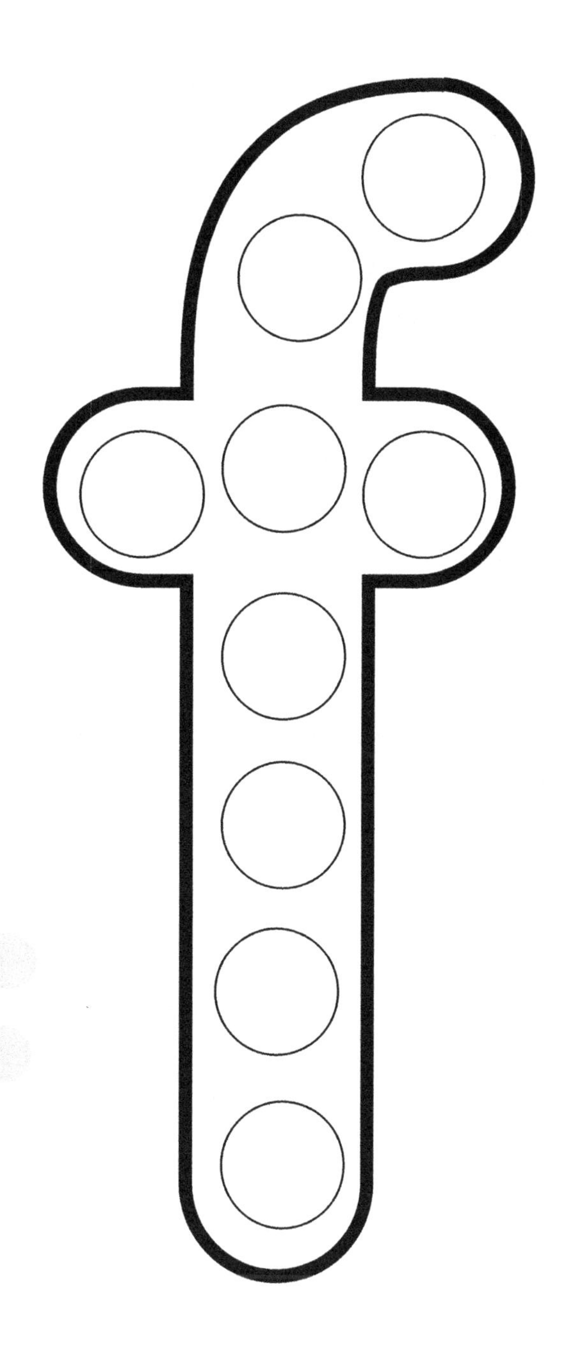

SLINKY
SLOTH

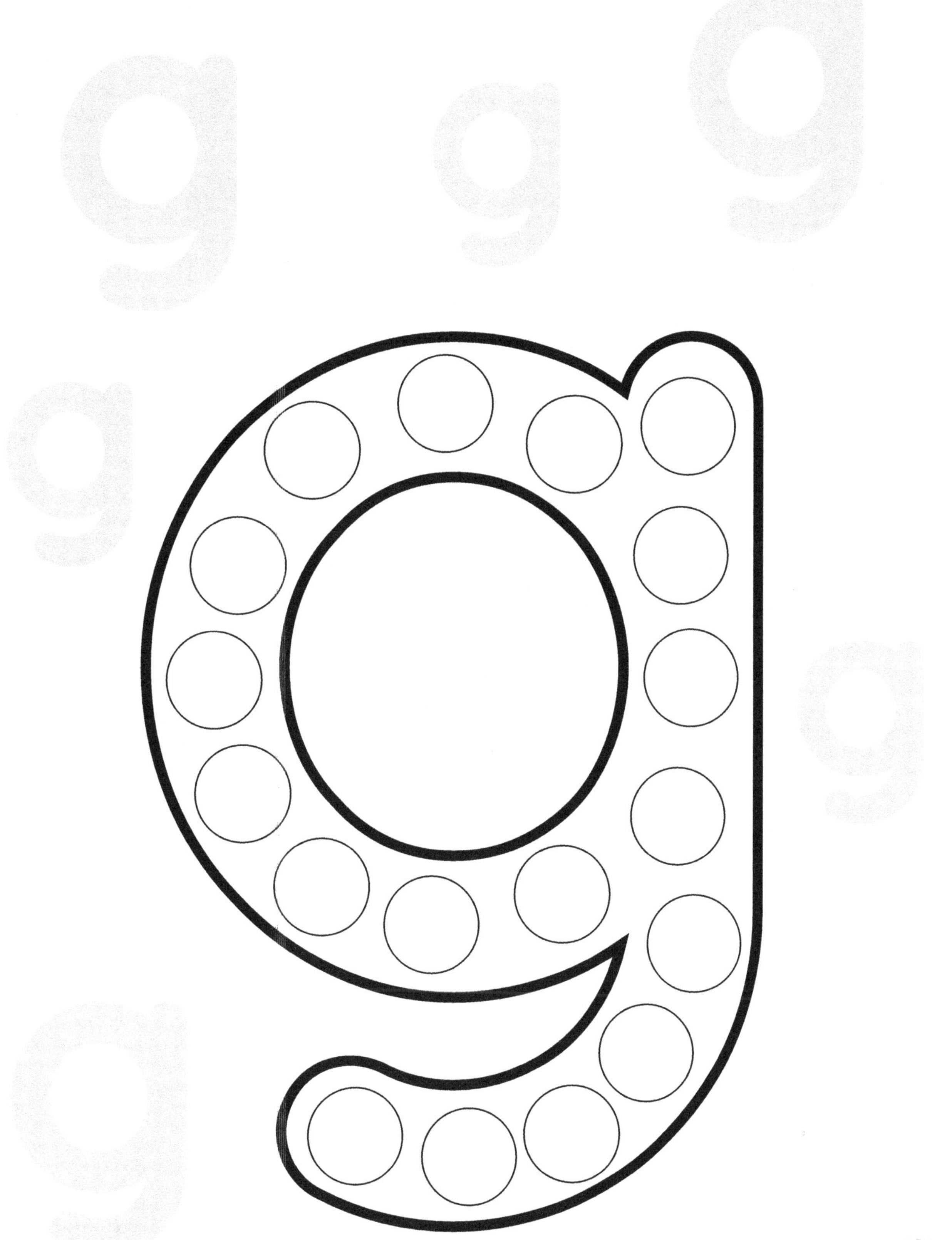

SLINKY
SLOTH

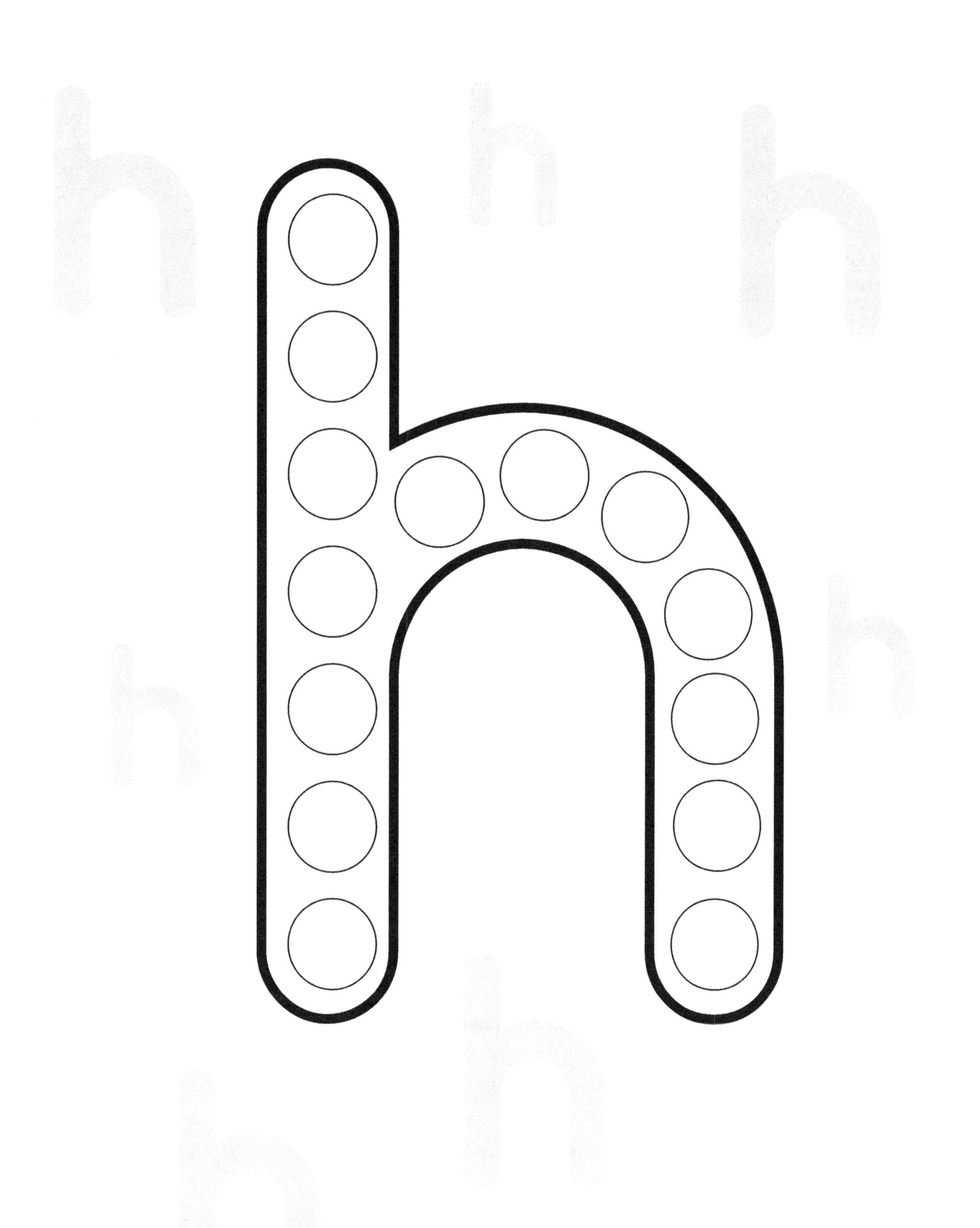

SLINKY
SLOTH

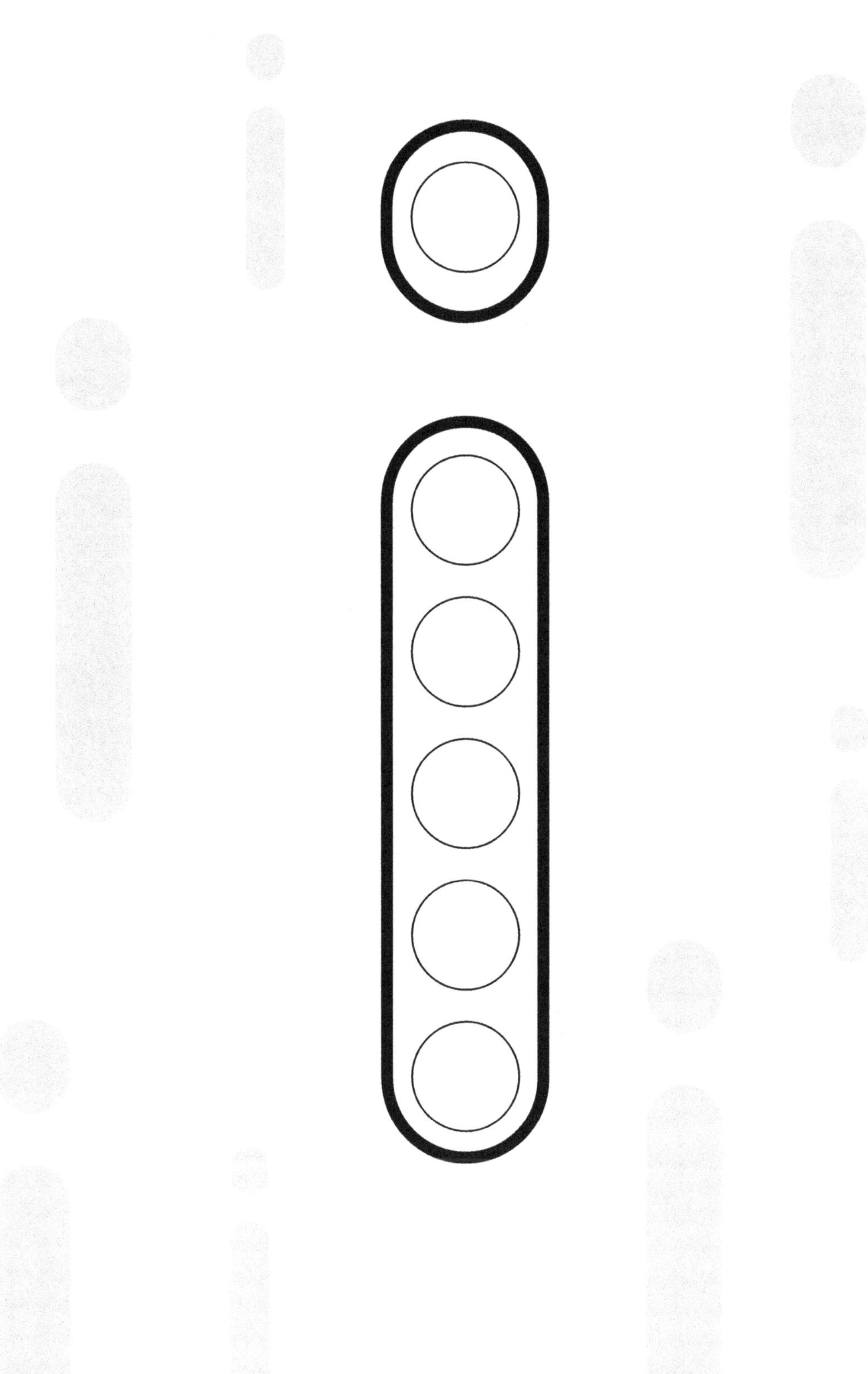

SLINKY
SLOTH

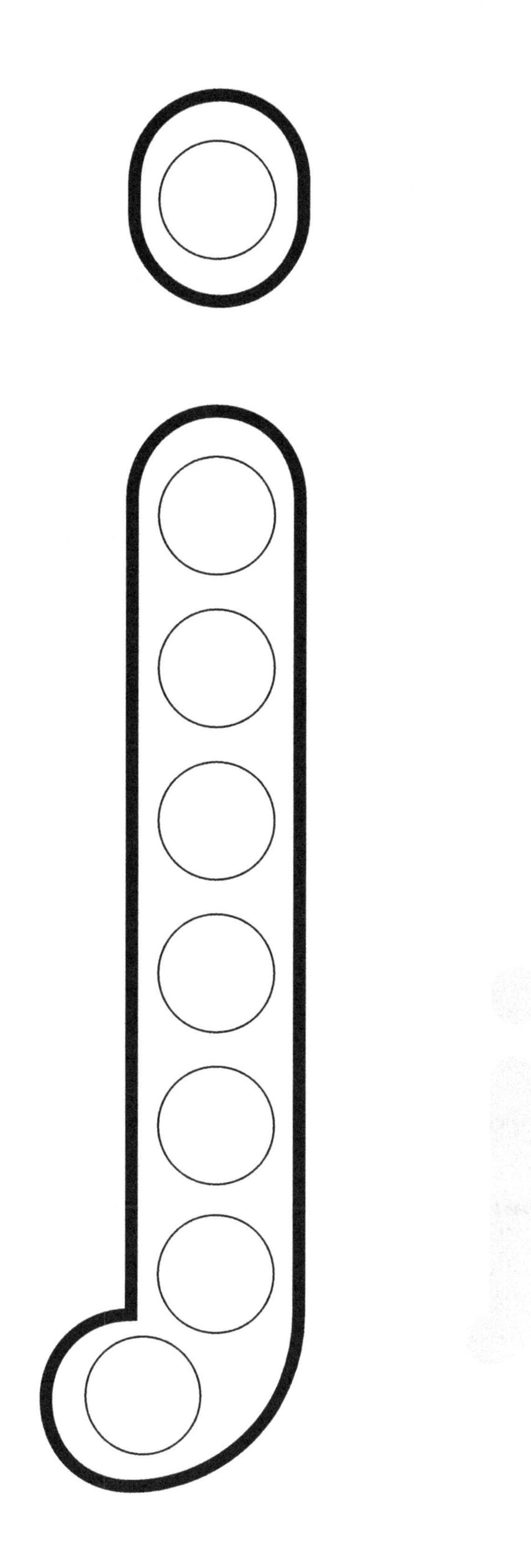

SLINKY
SLOTH

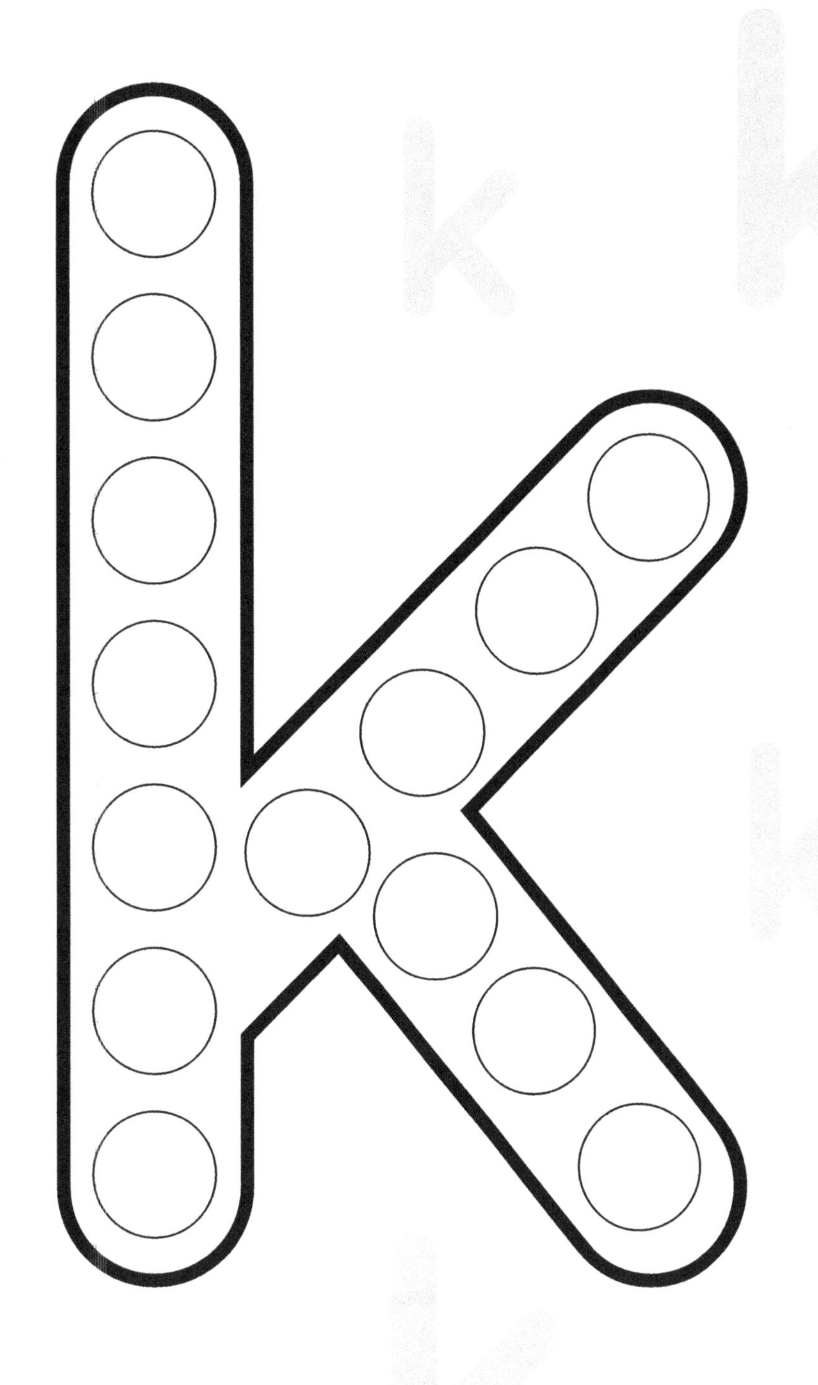

SLINKY
SLOTH

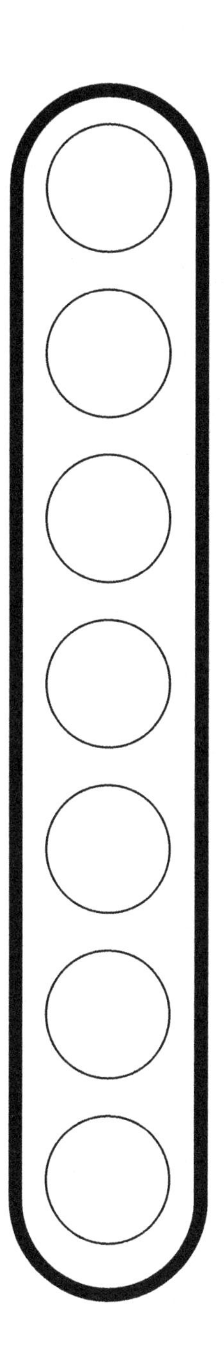

SLINKY
SLOTH

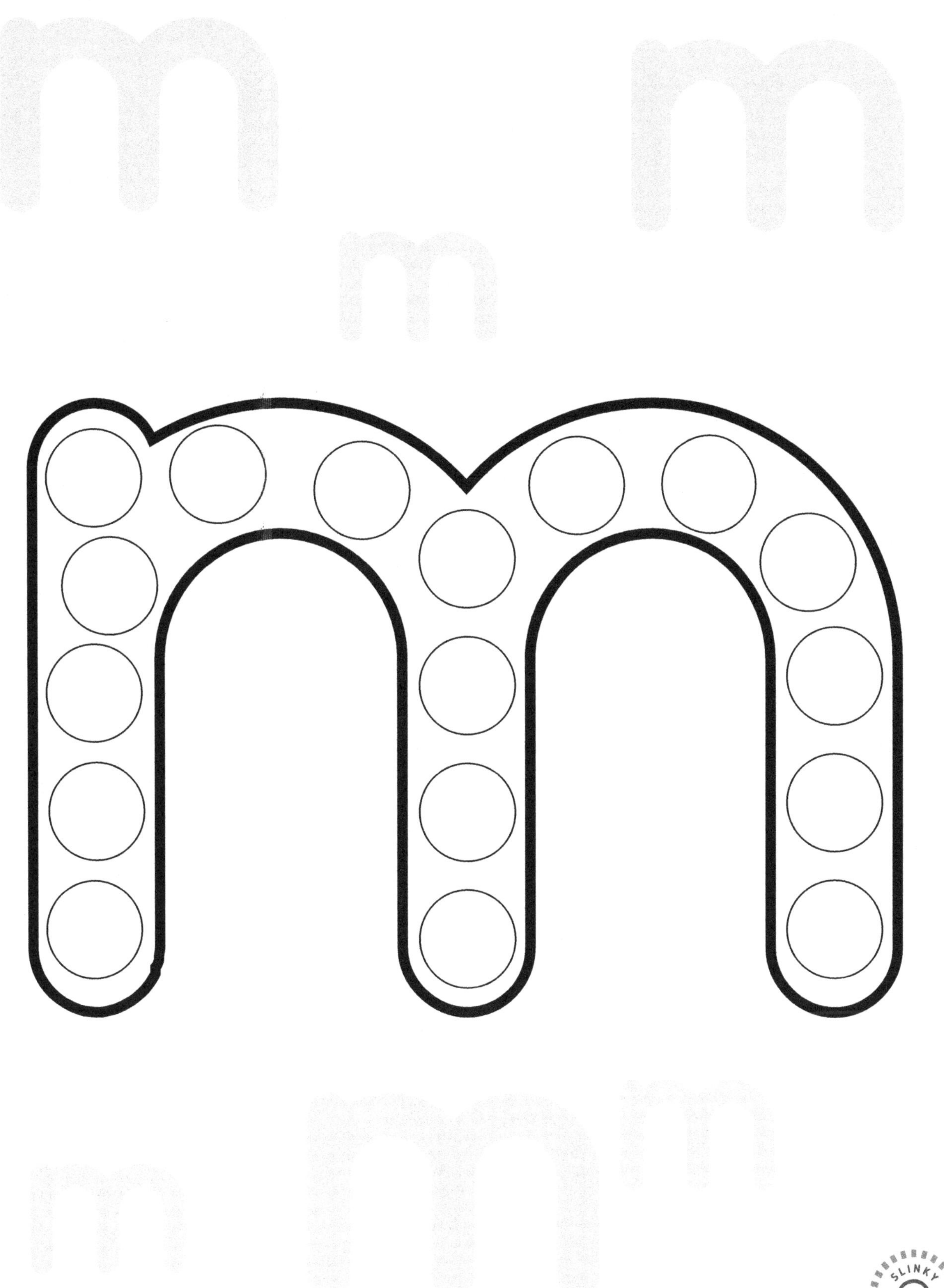

SLINKY
SLOTH

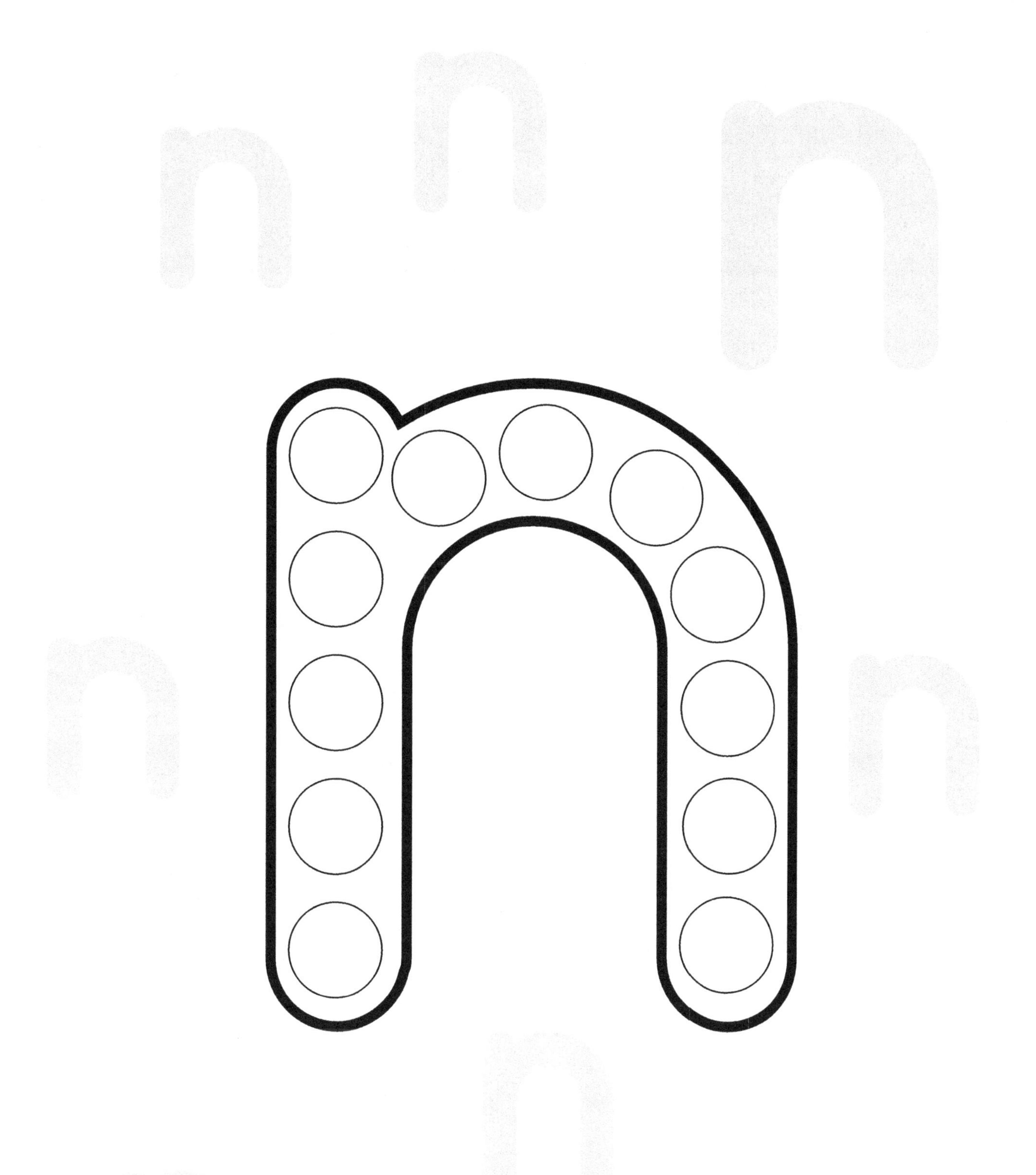

SLINKY
SLOTH

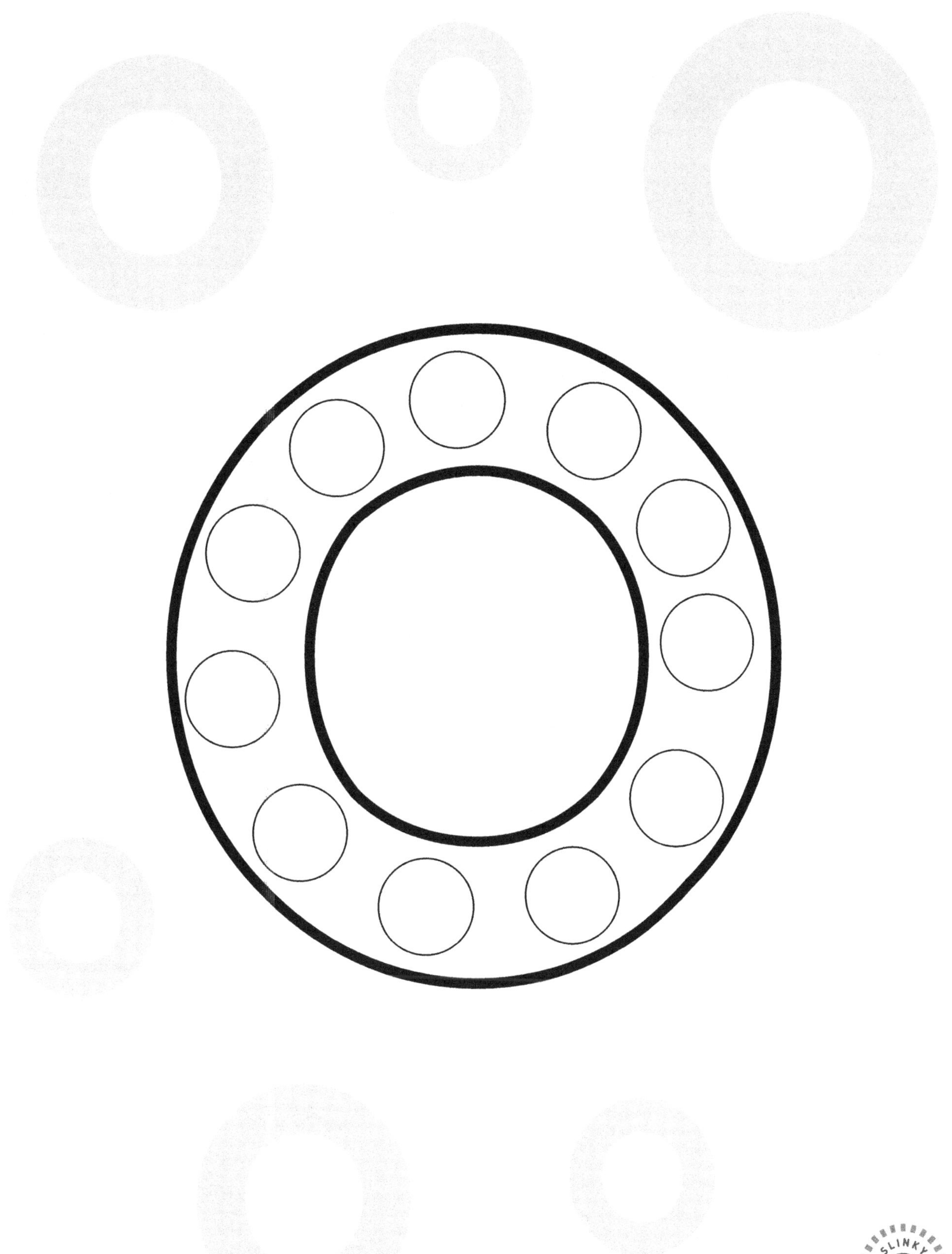

SLINKY
SLOTH

SLINKY
SLOTH

SLINKY
SLOTH

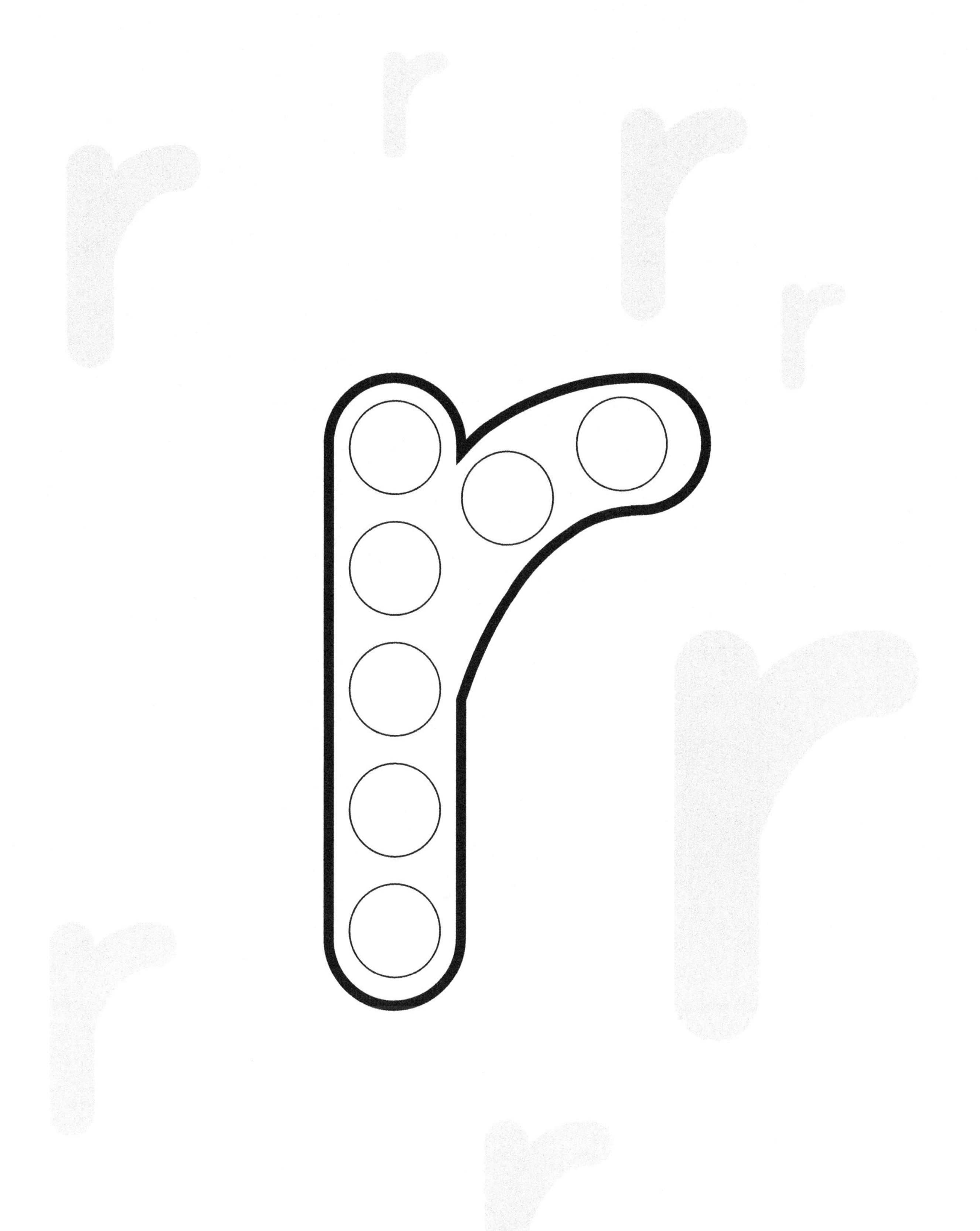

SLINKY
SLOTH

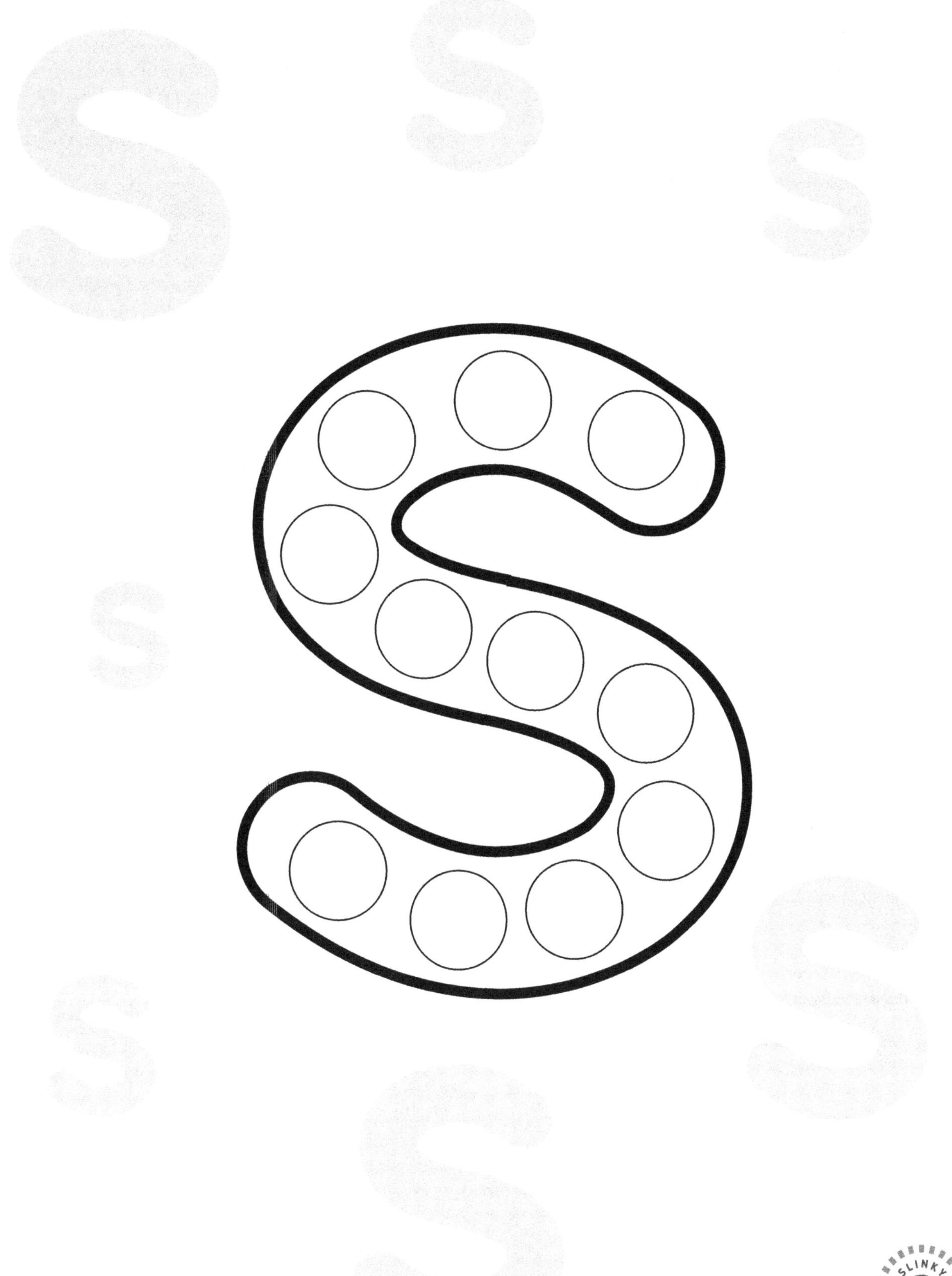

SLINKY
SLOTH

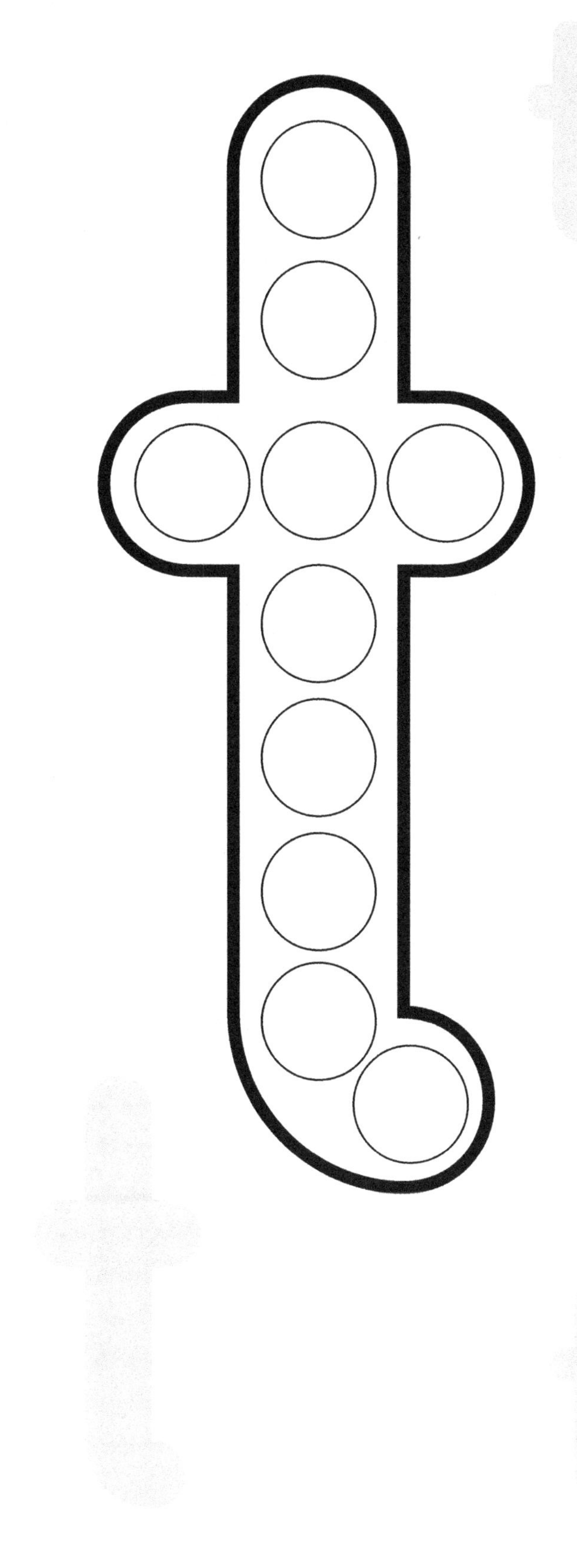

SLINKY
SLOTH

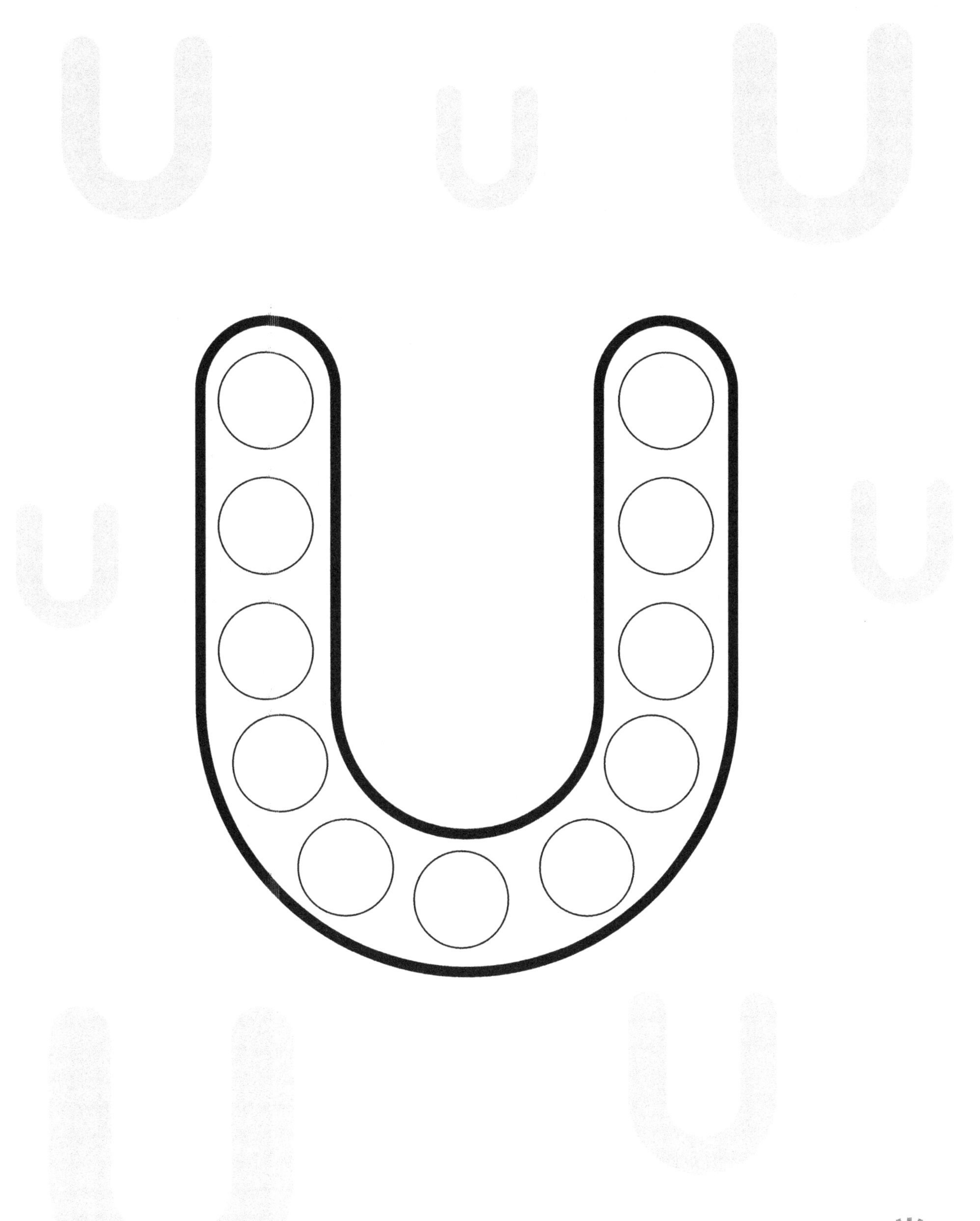

SLINKY
SLOTH

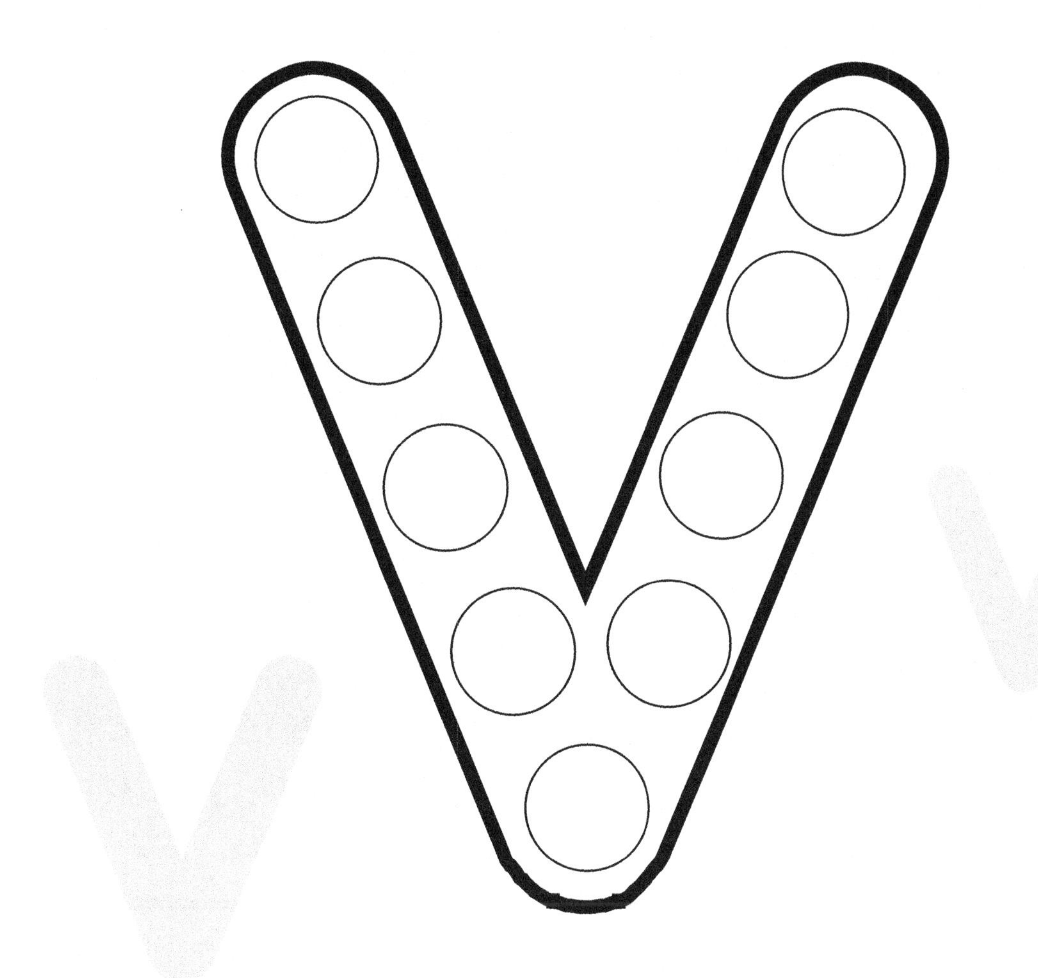

SLINKY
SLOTH

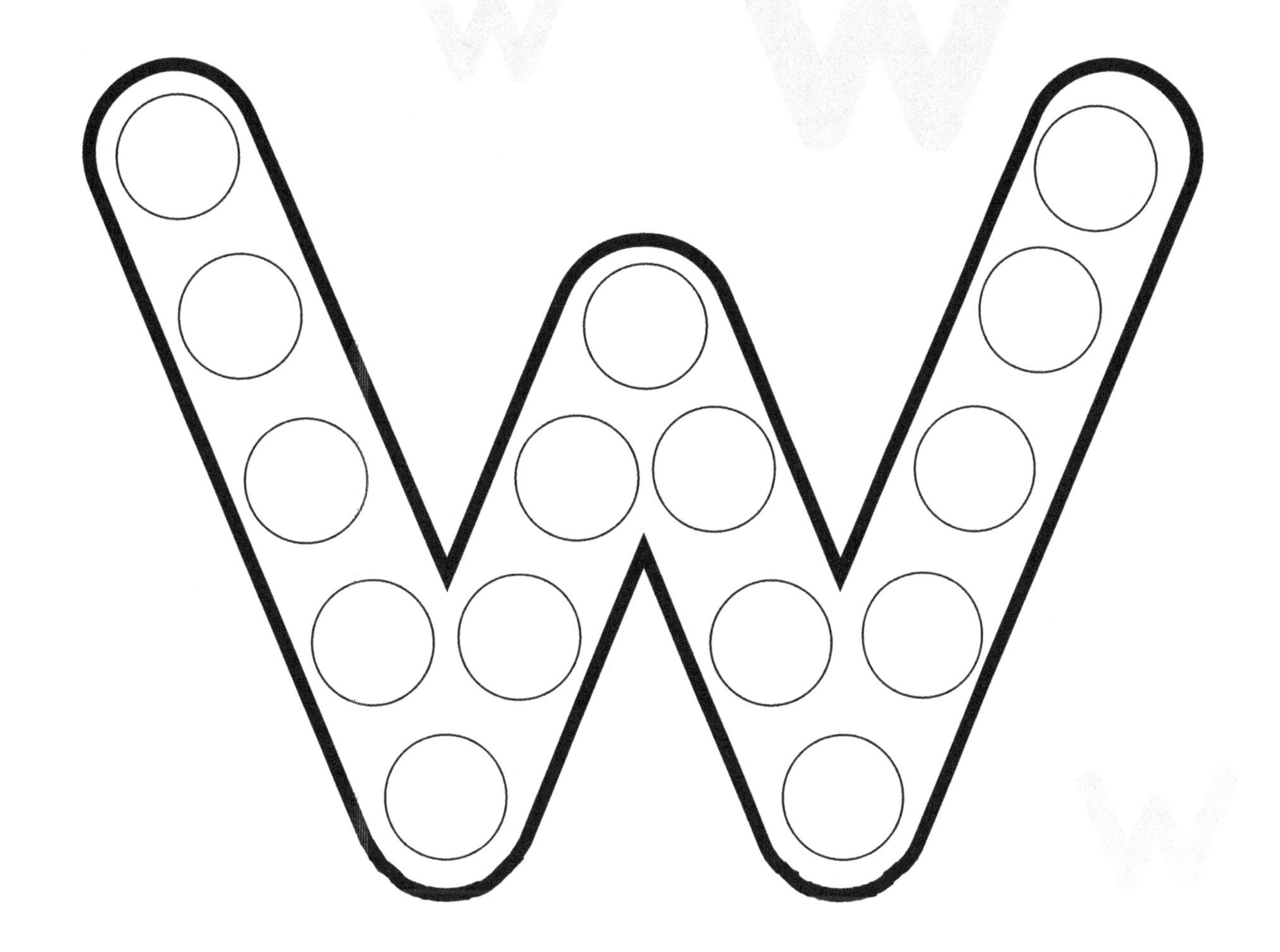

SLINKY
SLOTH

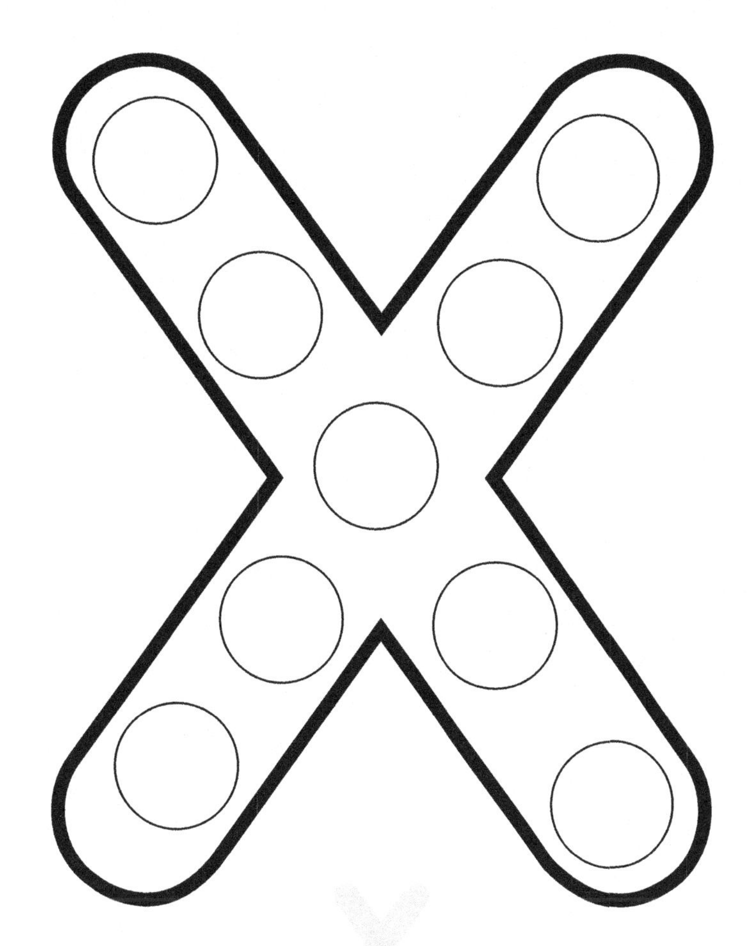

SLINKY
SLOTH

SLINKY
SLOTH

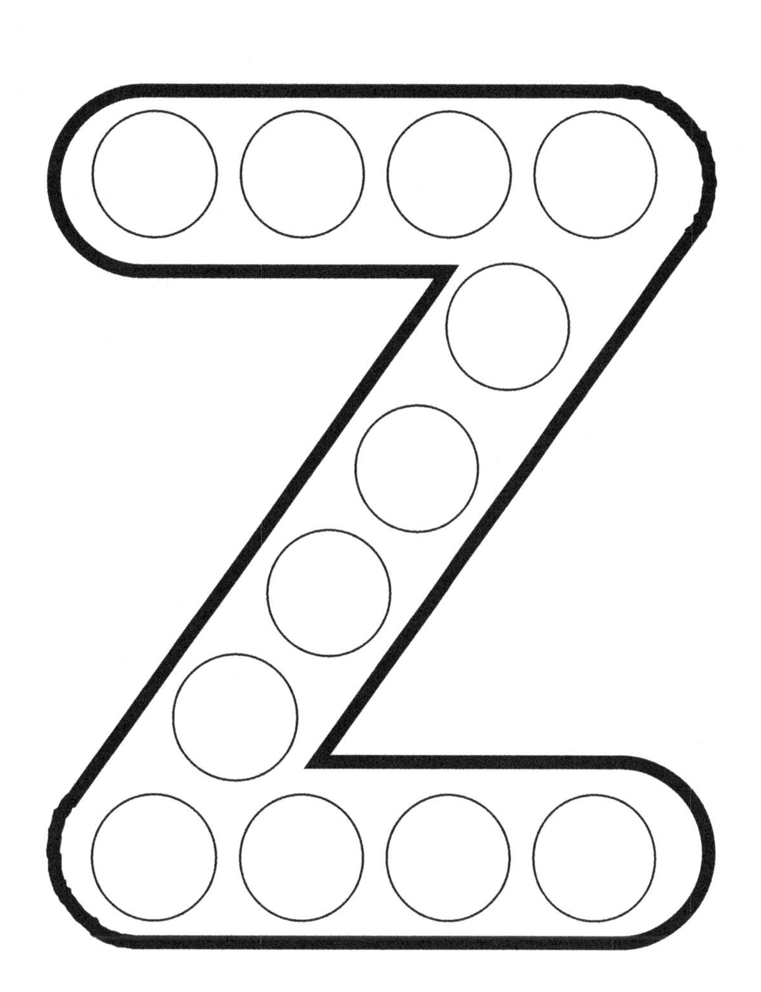

SLINKY
SLOTH

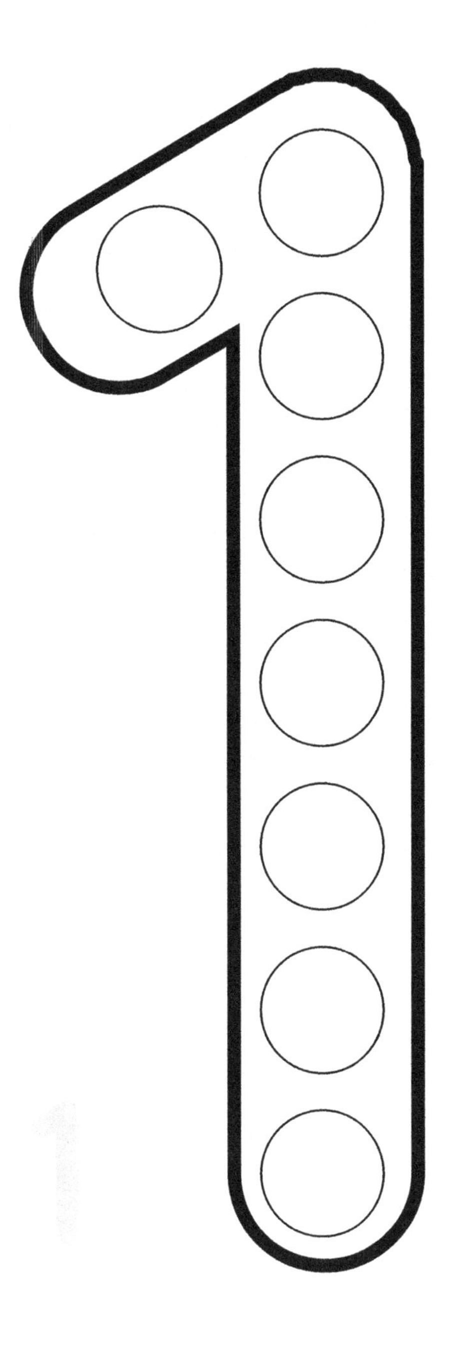

one

two

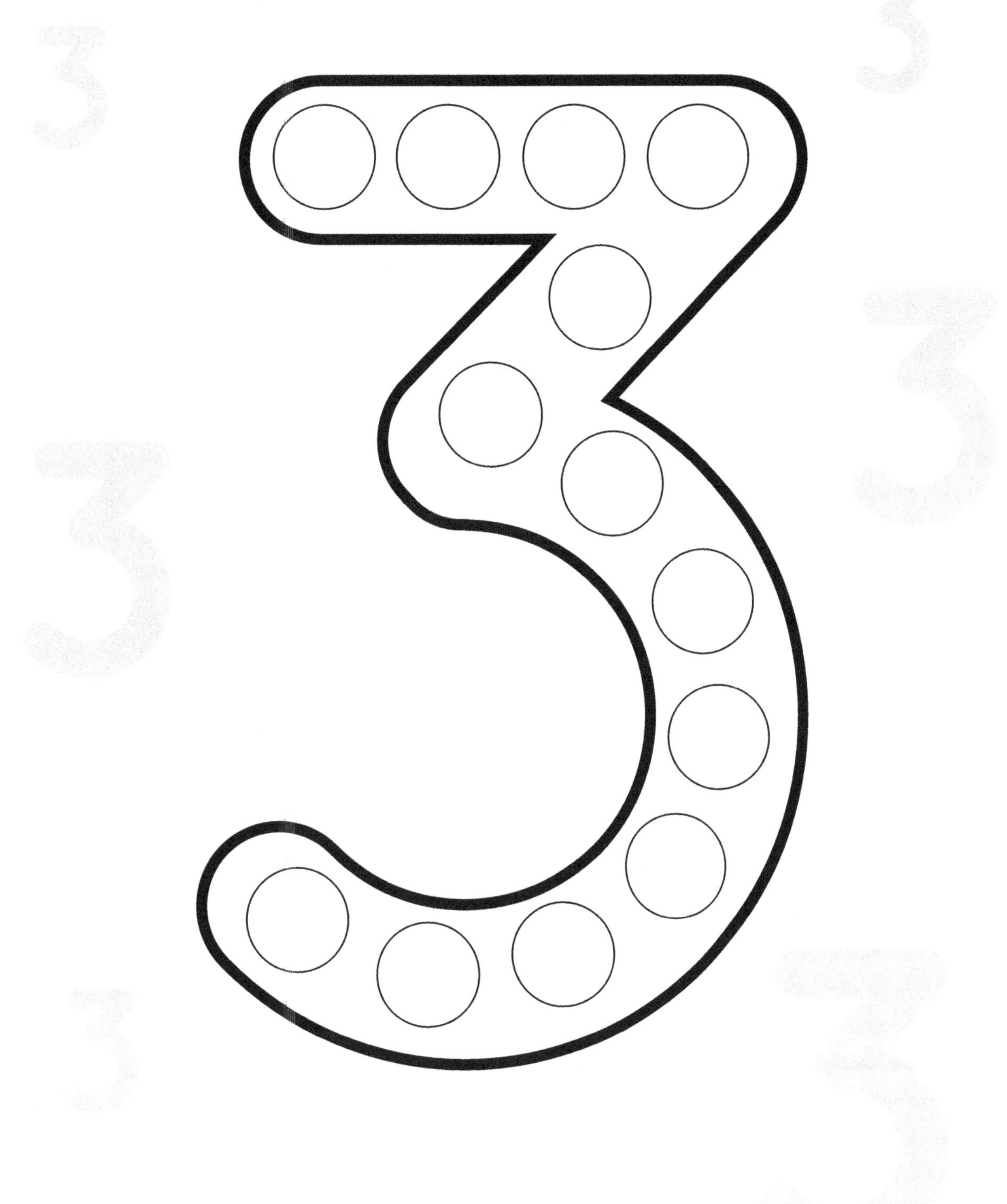

three

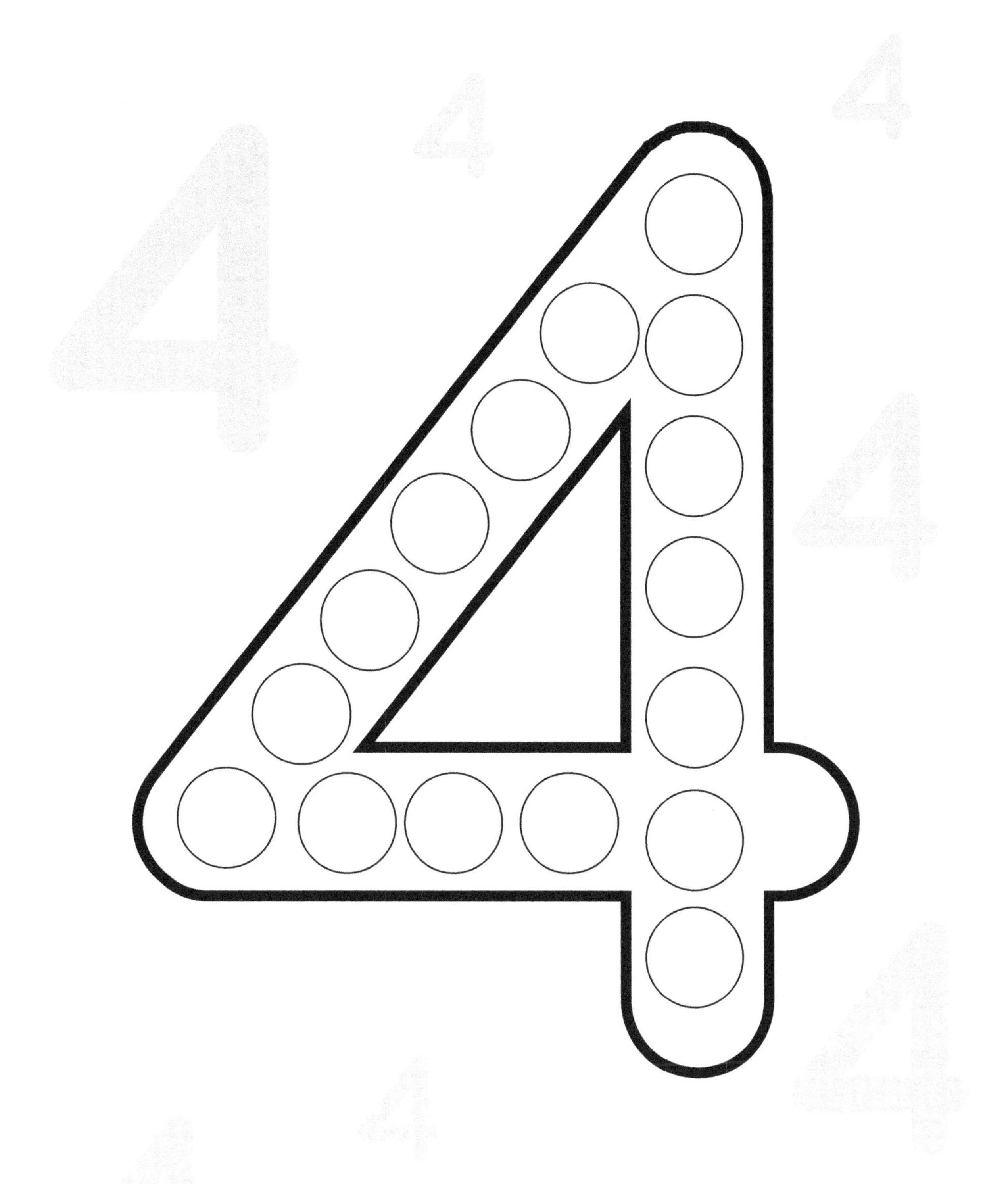

four

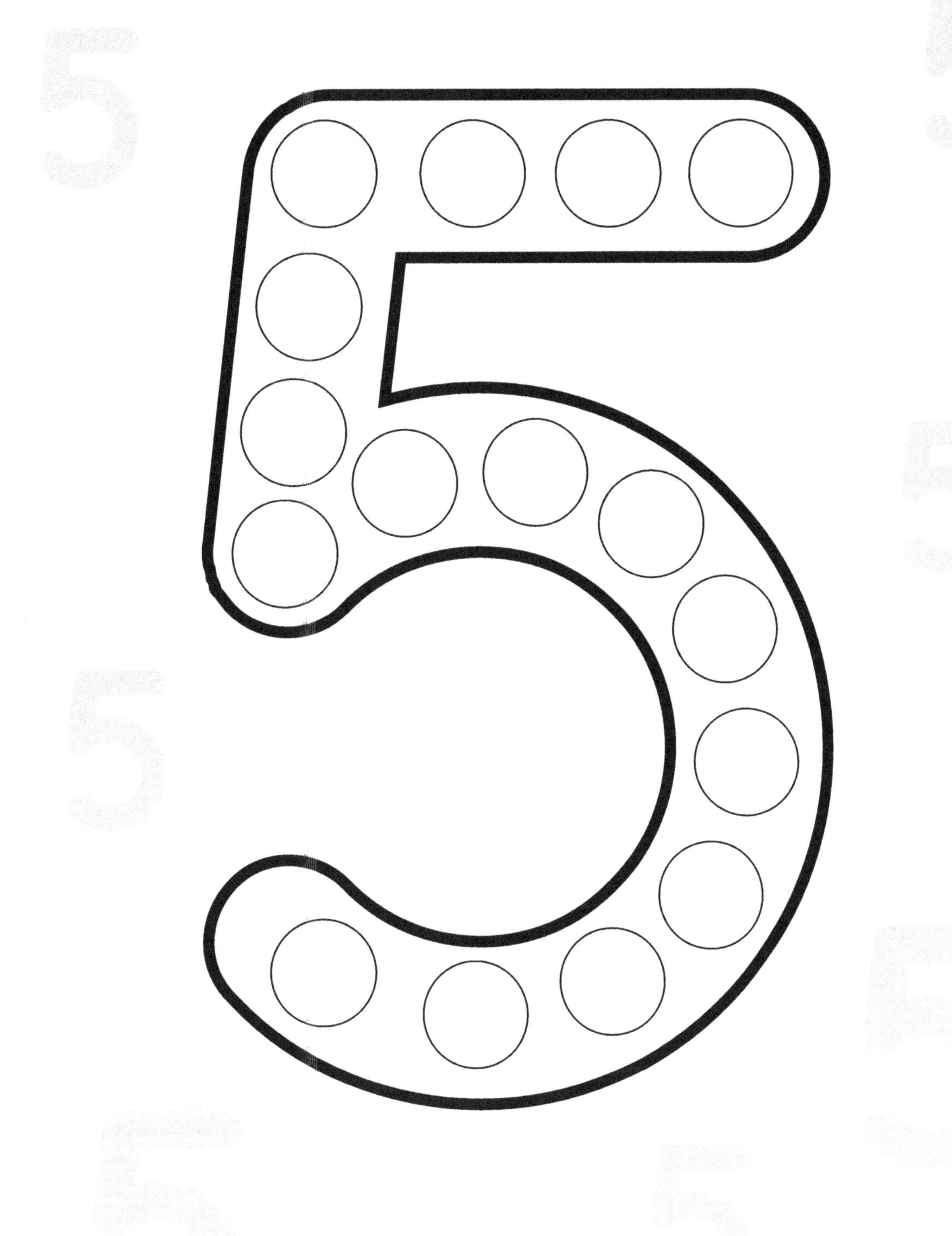

five

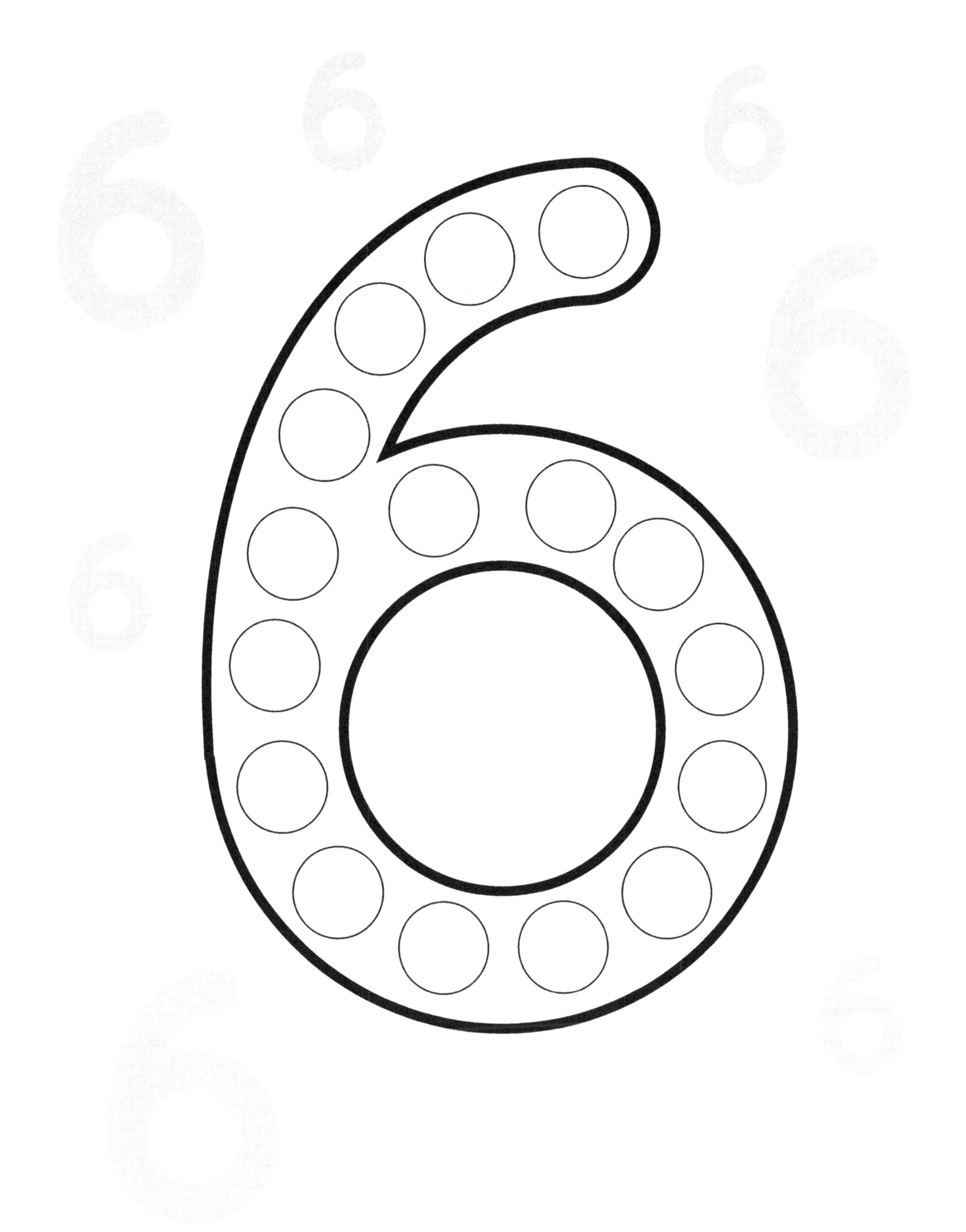

six

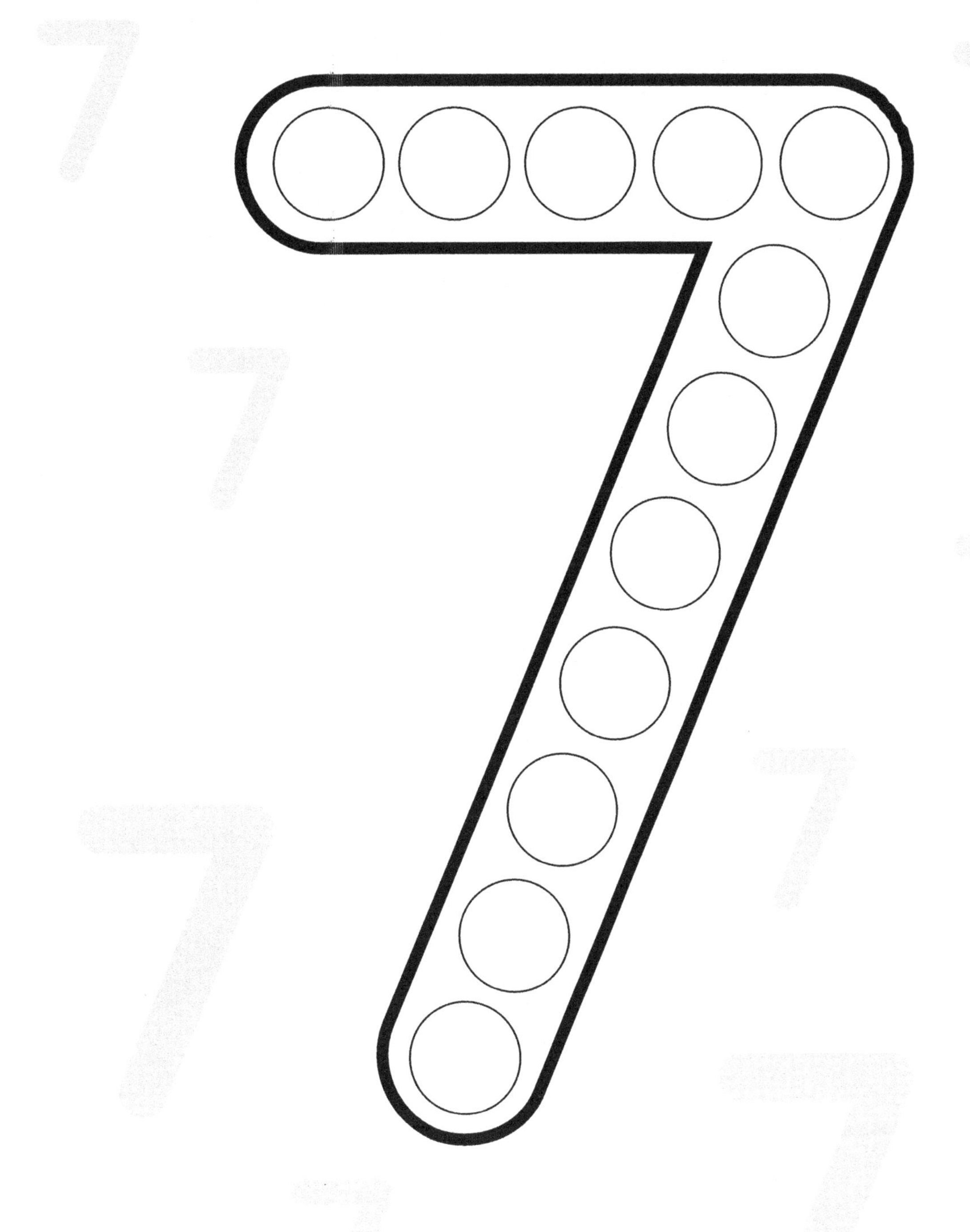

seven

eight

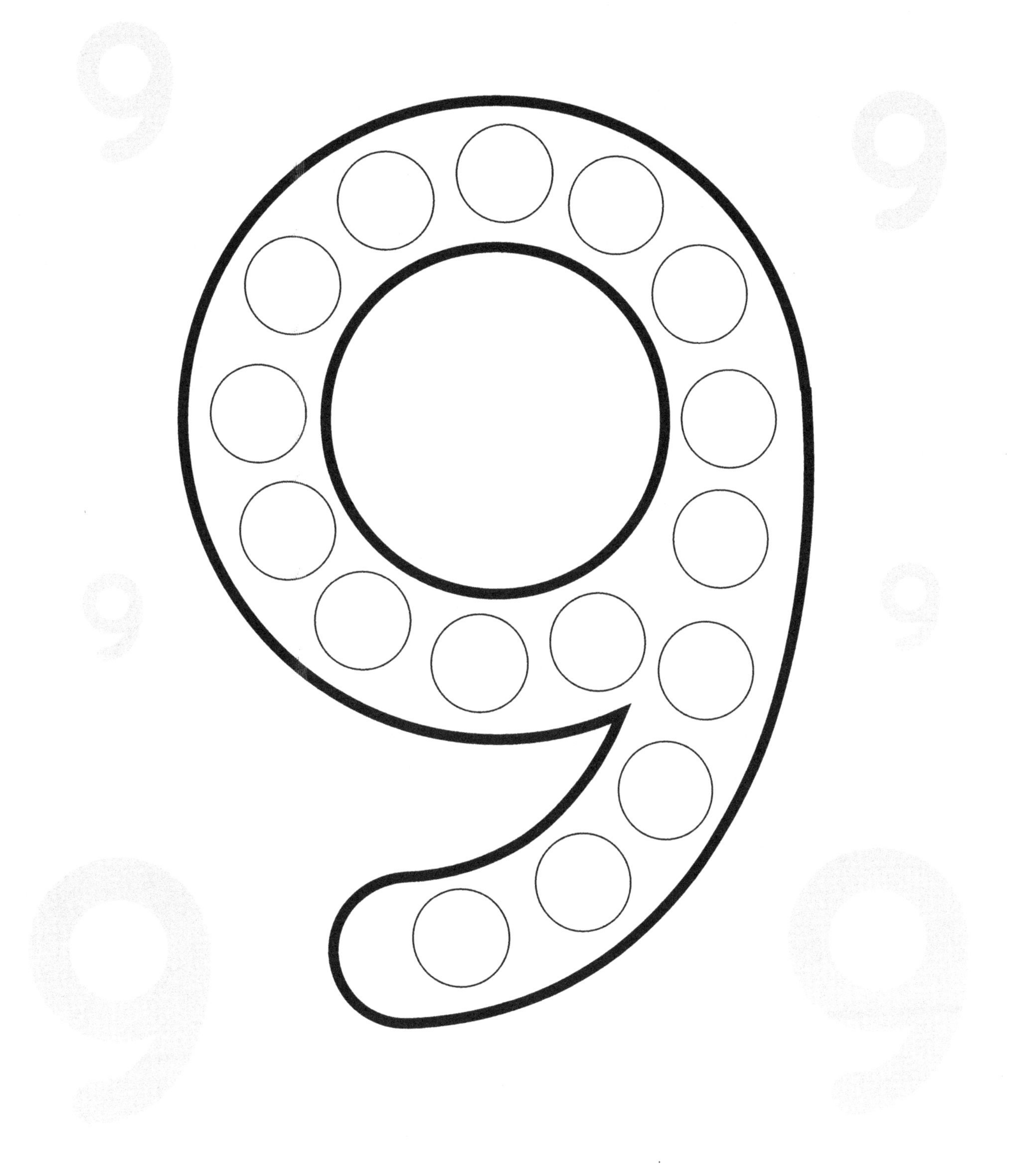

nine

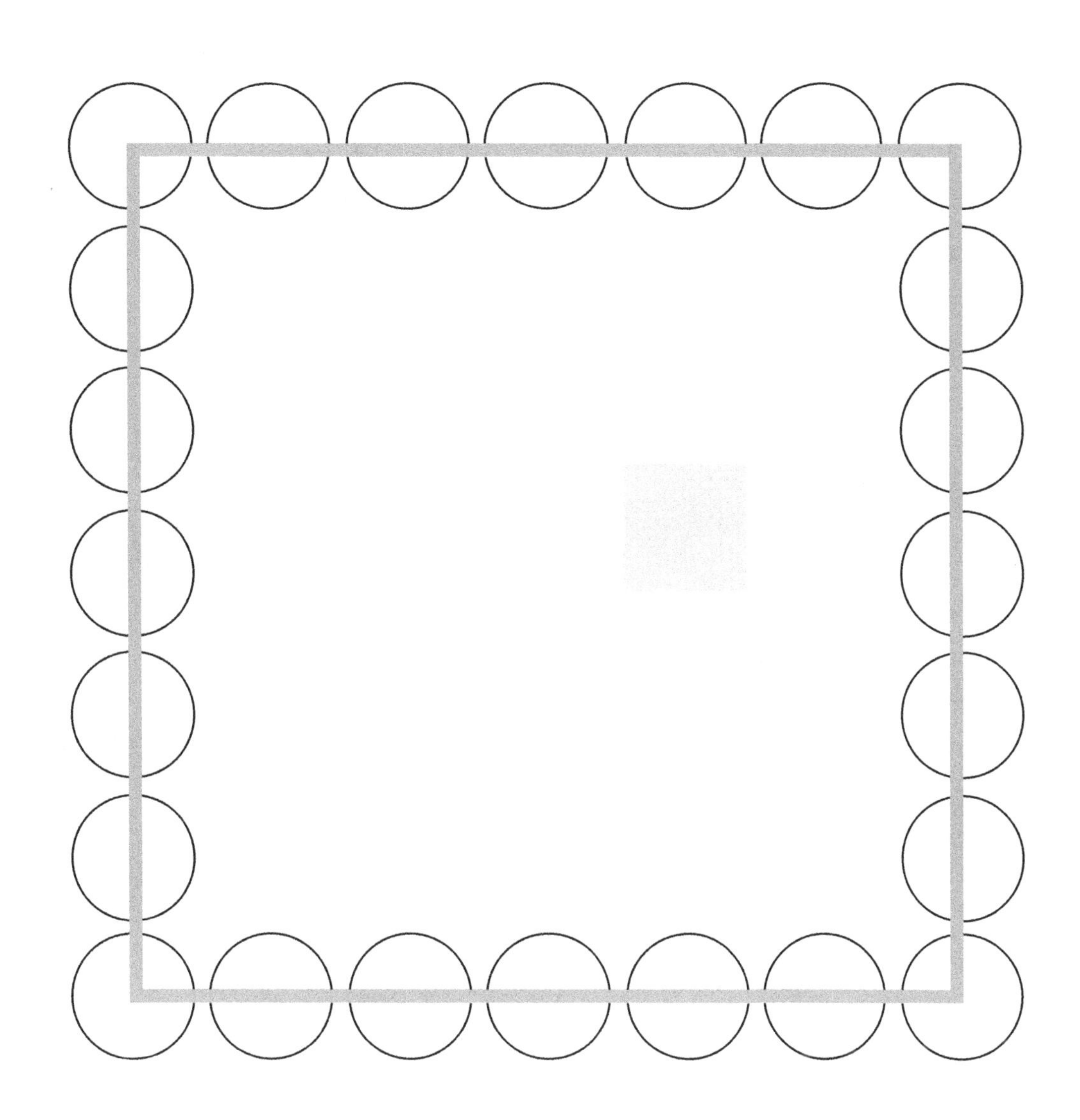

square

circle

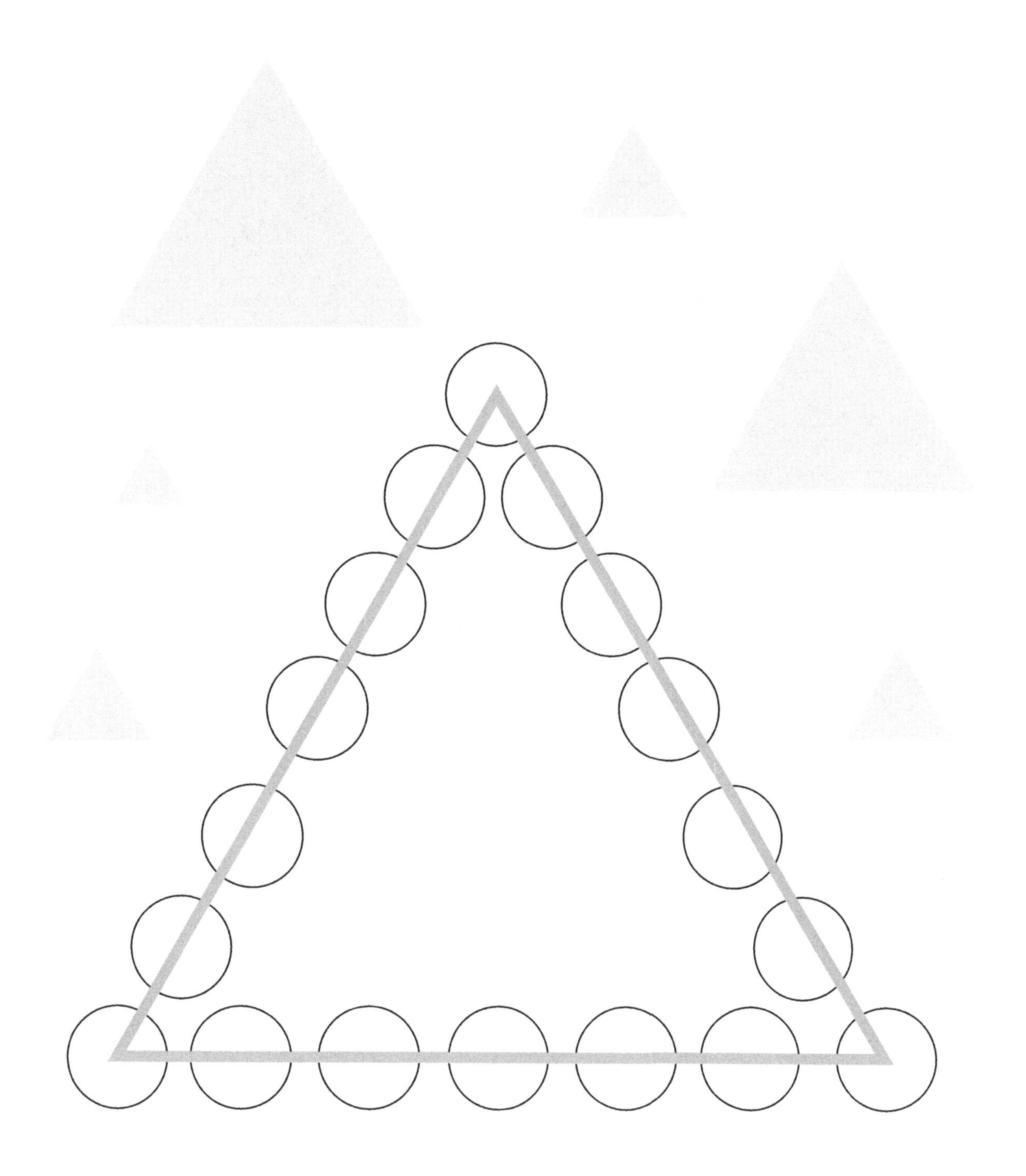

triangle

Made in the USA
Coppell, TX
14 June 2022